CW00670726

From Pain 2 Purpose is such a timely book for these dark times i֊ prayer is that God uses it as a light to those who find themselves of despair.

Ray Comfort, co-host of an award-winnin_____ and author of more than ninety books

From Pain 2 Purpose is a powerful book that strikes a cord regarding the human condition. We all experience pain, some at a deep level. Bearing their souls to tell their story, the Mullets give hope for people suffering all types of pain. The resounding yes of this book is the hope that it offers, even in the midst of the most tragic times.

Jay and Laura Laffoon, founders of Celebrate Ministries, speakers, and authors of numerous books, including *Celebrate Your Marriage*

There is counsel that comes from a book; it is helpful, clinical, and provides good information. There is also counsel that comes from a classroom; it is filled with wisdom and instruction. Then there is counsel that comes from the one who has walked where you are walking; been there, done that, you can survive, you can thrive, you can know joy again. *From Pain 2 Purpose* was written by a couple who have tasted the bitterness of loss and have chosen to take others by the hand and walk them through it. If your pain has stolen your sense of purpose, you really ought to consider allowing Duane and Cindy Mullett to share their walk through pain. You will realize you are not alone, and it will help you focus your eyes on the light at the end of your tunnel.

Michael Gantt, Michael Gantt Ministries, author, pastor, speaker, missionary

From Pain 2 Purpose is an honest reflection of a mother and father's struggle with the death of their sixteen-year-old son and the years of prolonged suffering he endured starting at five months of age. The entire family struggled with years of hospital visits, heart transplants, and then, to add to the battle, a bout with cancer. More suffering than anyone should have to endure! But they also share a path to healing and purpose, giving readers a method of "holding on...and letting go," using God's Word as the perfect teaching tool. This book is also structured to be helpful for a small group experience in healing from other loses, such as a job loss or divorce. The road for Duane and Cindy was not easy, but they have traveled it successfully. Thank you for sharing your story so others can heal.

Elaine Kennelly, author of *Finding Peace After a Suicide Loss: Healing Truths for Those Not Yet Healed*

The best reads are written from a place of deep experience. *From Pain 2 Purpose* is one of those heart-searching reads. It searches deep into the pain of loss, and teaches a clear path of redemption toward finding true purpose in pain and loss. Grieving the deep feelings of the heart over what is lost is never easy, but it can be redemptive. Thank you, Mulletts, for sharing your vulnerability and journey with all of us so we can move toward healing.

Stephen Stutzman, counselor, teacher, conference speaker, and founder and director of Strait Paths Foundation

We often equate brokenness to worthlessness, but in God's economy, something broken is most precious! Naturally, we run away from it, but God is drawn to it. When we invite the Healer into our brokenness, he makes beauty out of ashes. The Mullett family is a walking testimony of that. We've seen Duane and Cindy caring for those who are walking through painful times. They are genuine in their love and compassion for others. Knowing the deepness of the Father's love through walking their own journey of loss and unique situations, they pass that on in a way few people can. *From Pain 2 Purpose* is one way the Mulletts share what they have learned so that others can benefit.

Amos and Margaret Raber, ByGrace Ministries, authors, co-pastors, musicians, artists

Duane and Cindy write about grief and pain with a depth of understanding that could only be born from their own journey through pain. They share their story with a raw vulnerability that will move readers to tears, but the final message is one of redemptive purpose. Rather than empty clichés, the authors offer proven, biblical advice for anyone looking to take the first steps toward healing. I believe this book will be a valued resource for individuals and groups who need help navigating their own journey *From Pain 2 Purpose*.

Andrew Weaver, author, teacher

from **pain**

*2***purpose**

Rediscovering Joy
after Suffering a Major Loss

Duane and Cindy Mullett
with Dr. David Ferguson

BroadStreet
PUBLISHING

BroadStreet Publishing® Group, LLC
Savage, Minnesota, USA
BroadStreetPublishing.com

From Pain 2 Purpose: The Process of Recovering from Major Loss
Copyright © 2021 Duane and Cindy Mullett and the Great Commandment Network

978-1-4245-6252-7 (softcover)
978-1-4245-6253-4 (e-book)

Stock or custom editions of BroadStreet Publishing titles may be purchased in bulk for educational, business, ministry, fundraising, or sales promotional use. For information, please email orders@broadstreetpublishing.com.

Design and typesetting | garborgdesign.com

Printed in the United States of America

21 22 23 24 25 5 4 3 2 1

This book is lovingly dedicated in memory of our son, Austin, and to Dave and Becky Bellis's daughter, Denise. You are forever in our hearts, and both of you are continuing to impact many lives through your passing. We love you and will see you soon.

Contents

Section One

There Is Comfort for You to Receive

Section Two

There Are Promises for You to Claim

Section Three

There Is a Purpose God Wants to Reveal

Section Four

Other Losses

Introduction

From Pain 2 Purpose is designed to bring a fresh perspective to what it means to recover from major loss and heal unresolved grief. The goal of this resource is to help you move beyond knowing and understanding the need to "press on" and move toward what it means to persevere in tribulation, grieve with hope, and trust in the Lord (1 Thessalonians 4:13; Romans 12:12; Psalm 9:10). As you will see, when you deepen your own experience of God's love and care, you will be better equipped to let go of any unresolved grief and hold onto the hope of our Savior. You will stand more firmly on the truth that our hope is in him (Psalm 62:5).

This resource is also about relationships—the relationship with yourself, a relationship with a loved one you may have lost, your relationship with a trusted journey partner, and your relationship with Jesus. This kind of focus requires a relational faith—because it is only that kind of faith that produces hope and freedom.

In order to fully illustrate what a relational faith includes, we have defined forty different Spirit-empowered outcomes and categorized them into four themes (see Appendices 2 and 3). A Spirit-empowered disciple:

- Loves the Lord (L1–10): Here you will find specific times for expression of your love for Jesus and experience his care for you.

- Lives His Word (W1–10): These moments will equip you in how to live out specific Scriptures from God's Word.

- Loves People (P1–P10): These outcomes are specifically noted within the text but are also reflected throughout the personal assignments you complete on your own and then share with your journey partner. It's in these moments you will both give and receive care because of your connection with God's people.

- Lives His Mission (M1–10): These outcomes reflect the testimony of hope that will be yours as you complete the journey within this resource. After you have come to a greater place of healing, you will be better equipped to share Jesus' love with others and live out your purpose of telling others about the one who lives inside of you.

And each Spirit-empowered outcome will be noted with the following symbol:

Our world needs more people living as Spirit-empowered disciples who are making disciples who, in turn, make disciples. Thus, *From Pain 2 Purpose* rightly focuses on the powerful simplicity of…

- Receiving God's love for us and then gratefully expressing our love to him in return.

- Living his Word—because there's power and possibility in experiencing Scripture.

- Loving people by developing a lifestyle of vulnerability and genuine faith with other believers.

- Living his mission, which means building a lasting legacy as you share Jesus' hope with others.

As you read through this resource, we invite you to walk:

- In the light of God's Son as you *Encounter Jesus* (see John 8:12 and the corresponding headings)

- In the light of God's Word as you *Experience Scripture* (see Psalm 119:105 and the corresponding headings)

- In the light of God's people as you *Engage in Fellowship* through vulnerably sharing with your journey partner (see Matthew 5:14)

We encourage you to find a trusted friend, family member, counselor, pastor, or small group member who will become your designated journey partner as you work through this resource. Since we are better equipped to walk in the light when we are accompanied by God's people, and because it is not good for us to be alone, we consider it critical for you to have at least one person who will walk with you in this grief journey (Genesis 2:18). We'll be praying for God's provision of at least one trusted person who will listen and care.

You will also find a Pain 2 Purpose Group Leaders Guide at the end of this book. It is our hope that you and/or your journey partner might so benefit from the biblical truths of this resource that you gratefully pass them on to others. The Pain 2 Purpose Group Leaders Guide provides a suggested outline for facilitating this resource with members of a small group.

Finally, the Great Commandment Network's resource development team serves various partners as they work faithfully to equip others in a lifestyle of hope and healing. Towards this goal, we are thrilled to serve our ministry partners, Duane and Cindy Mullett. We hope the sections identified as Encounter Jesus, Experience Scripture, and Engage in Fellowship will provide you with a hope-filled path to purpose. May Jesus richly bless each person who makes the journey *From Pain 2 Purpose.*

Terri Snead

Executive Editor

Great Commandment Network

1

I Can't Let Go!

"Something's wrong, Duane. Austin is barely breathing!"

I (Cindy) was seated up front in the motorhome holding my five-month-old son. He had just gone to sleep when his body suddenly went completely limp in my arms. Alarmed, I shook him gently. "Austin! Austin! Wake up!" I cried. No response. He quit breathing. Now fighting panic, I started to blow in his face to get him to breathe, but there was still no response. Duane, my husband, was driving. He made an immediate U-turn and headed straight back to the only place he knew to go: the doctor's office we had just left. We were in Columbia, South Carolina, in the midst of a ministry tour. Duane was part of a singing group, and I assisted at the ministry's resource table. The day before, we were to conduct an evening church event, and I had noticed that little Austin had been sleeping a lot during the day. As the day wore on, I noticed he looked a bit pale. By evening Austin's breathing became faster, and he was fussier than normal. He also began running a low-grade fever.

The following morning, we took Austin to an urgent care facility where a doctor diagnosed an ear infection and put our baby on an antibiotic. He attributed his rapid breathing to the fever. Encouraged that Austin's condition was not serious, we confidently headed out of town for another meeting that evening.

But now in emergency mode, we were racing back to the doctor. By now Austin's eyes were rolling back into his head and his little fingernails were turning blue. I opened the window and held his face close to it to give him as much oxygen as possible.

Duane took the first exit off the interstate, but seeing Austin's deteriorating condition, he realized that we would not reach the doctor's office in time. Abandoning all caution, he jumped a curb to get to a gas station. Taking Austin from my arms, he rushed inside the building.

"Please call 911!" he cried in panic to the clerk. As the clerk dialed the number, I heard Duane cry out desperately, "O Lord, help us! Please save Austin!" When the 911 operator came on the line, Duane quickly explained the situation to her. She began asking him questions. "Can anyone there perform CPR?"

No one could.

"Do the best you can to keep him breathing," she said. "Help is on the way."

I had followed Duane into the store and watched helplessly as he laid Austin on the counter and began trying to give him CPR. Neither Duane nor I had ever been trained in CPR, but Duane did the best he could. He pressed repeatedly on Austin's tiny chest and blew into his mouth, attempting to inflate his lungs. Thankfully, Austin began to revive a bit.

An ambulance arrived quickly. As the driver and young male medic loaded Austin into the ambulance, a female paramedic I had not previously seen said she was going with me. Without another word, she ushered me into the ambulance, which immediately rushed toward the hospital. Duane followed behind in the motorhome.

Minutes after the journey began, Austin's condition warranted a Code Blue. Frantic with fear, I watched in helpless horror as my baby's body began to shut down. For some reason, the male medic froze up. He seemed paralyzed, as if in shock, unable to do anything. Immediately the woman took charge. "Mama," she said, looking straight at me, "Talk to your baby. Touch him. Let him know you are there. He needs to hear your voice!" Even as she spoke, her hands were flying back and forth between Austin and the equipment in the ambulance. She seemed to know exactly what to do to support Austin as he kept going in and out of consciousness. She kept working, and I kept talking to Austin all the way to the hospital.

When the ambulance arrived, the medical staff took Austin straight to the ICU. After both Duane and I had endured several hours of anxious, prayerful waiting, a doctor came out and gave us the diagnosis. "Austin has cardiomyopathy, which is an enlarging of the heart."

"What caused it?" I asked.

"A virus, most likely. We're not sure," the doctor replied. "But one thing is certain; the damage to your baby's heart is so extensive that it will not sustain his life much longer. He will need a heart transplant—and soon."

Duane and I stood speechless. Finally, Duane spoke up.

"Can we see our son?"

The doctor nodded and led us into the ICU.

A devastating sight met our eyes. Our tiny son was hooked up to a whole array of machines. He was on a ventilator with multiple IVs and monitors attached to him. He was fully sedated so that he couldn't move. It would be seven days before I could even hold Austin again.

Prior to this I would have said I had a perfect life. I was seventeen years old when I first saw Duane. He was twenty-two and performing as a guitarist and vocalist in a Christian singing group. Duane was good looking, had a wonderful singing voice, and he came across as a gentle kind of guy.

Two years later I got a secretarial job at the same ministry office where Duane worked. Though Duane and I chatted from time to time, I really didn't think he was that interested in me. But he was. Eventually he asked me out, and after a year-long courtship, we got married. Like any young bride, I had utopian dreams for our life together. I wanted a large, happy family that would travel together in Christian service, singing and ministering the gospel to those who needed it most. After two years of marriage, our son Austin was born. I felt like I had the perfect family. I was serving God with the love of my life and nurturing a beautiful, healthy baby boy. I didn't think it could get any better than that. Then this happened. And I had no idea that "this" was only the beginning of an emotional roller coaster ride with Austin being in and out of the hospital for years, our daughter also needing a heart transplant, and many other severe health issues. Then came the devastating blow: the death of our only son.

The Faces of Grief

If you have just suffered a major loss, you have probably begun the emotional roller coaster ride of feeling your own grief. Your grief—which descends on you as overwhelming feelings of loss—can reveal itself through several faces that can leave you suffering in any number of ways. Here are a few.

> *Suffering a major loss can leave you with a broken heart.*

When you say you are heartbroken, you may be using a metaphor, but what you are experiencing is real suffering and grief. Heartbreak over a major loss causes excruciating pain. Overwhelming grief can make it hard to breathe. It can leave you physically and emotionally exhausted.

> *Suffering a major loss can leave you struggling spiritually with a lot of unanswered questions.*

Major losses usually make no sense—the loss of a home caused by fire, natural disasters, the divorce between two people who once loved each other, the death of a loved one, or a global tragedy like the coronavirus pandemic of 2020 that brought financial disaster, uncertainty, and loss to so many. It all seems so cruel, wrong, and unfair. You may even question where God is during all this. That's a natural response. Tragic losses tend to cause fear and shake one's faith.

> *Suffering a major loss can leave you feeling lost, alone, and incomplete.*

Grieving a deep loss can also shake you at the very core of your being. Suffering a loss, especially the loss of a loved one, can make you feel that a part of you has been torn away.

It can seem like your loss has left a hole in your heart. You may even feel a loss of identity, a sense of incompleteness, and the feeling that you are no longer a whole person. Emotionally disconnected, you may feel adrift, without an emotional anchor.

> *Suffering a major loss can leave you deprived of emotional peace of mind.*

Grieving can cause emotional distress. Disheartened, you may feel an inward discontentment and frustration. You may find it difficult to rest or sleep. The gnawing ache in your soul can sap the joy and peace out of life.

> *Suffering a major loss can leave you with a clouded sense of purpose.*

Grief-stricken, heartbroken, and disheartened, it's hard to imagine how to move forward in life after a major loss. Life may seem colorless. You may feel enveloped in an atmosphere of gloom, and it's hard to see past it. Tomorrow may show up, but it doesn't feel much like it offers you a meaningful future.

Rationally, you may know you must somehow move forward. Yet emotionally, the fog you're in may feel too overwhelming to try. If only you could reverse time and avoid the need to grieve. But you can't.

When our Austin died, what we personally needed as a family were the same things most people who are suffering a major loss need in order to move forward in life. Those common needs are *healing of a broken heart, spiritual strength, a renewed sense of wholeness, emotional peace of mind, and a renewed sense of purpose*. While all of that is eventually possible, none of us has been prepared in advance to obtain it. In fact, many get bogged down in their grief and find it very difficult to move forward.

Take the next few moments to stop and give yourself the time and emotional space to reflect on this question: What do you most need in order to move forward in life? Do you need more healing for your broken heart? A renewed sense of wholeness? More peace? A renewed sense of purpose? Or something else? Consider the promise of Jeremiah 29:11 and write your reflections below.

EXPERIENCE SCRIPTURE

"For I know the plans I have for you," says the Lord.
They are plans for good and not for disaster,
to give you a future and a hope."
Jeremiah 29:11

Lord, as I begin this journey from pain to purpose, I want this promise of a "future and a hope" to be real in my life. I am asking you to make it so.

In order to move forward in life, I need…

I'm trusting you for a fresh future and renewed hope.

 W10. A Spirit-empowered disciple has an implicit, unwavering trust that his Word will never fail.

Unresolved Grief

Experiencing losses is a part of life. They should be expected, yet it is not easy to anticipate or cope with them. As a child, you may have suffered the loss of friendships, losses in sporting events, the loss of a pet, or even the devastating loss that came from your parents' divorce. While such losses are inevitable in a fallen world, we seem unprepared to deal with them adequately. It seems we must find ways of coping with them even as we face them.

You or someone you know may have recently experienced a loss—the loss of health, the loss of a friend or family member through death, the loss of a job, loss of a business, the loss of financial stability, a loss due to a divorce, or the loss of a home through a natural disaster. In each case, that loss, whether small or great, causes grief and pain.

For example, so many have felt the impact of COVID-19. It has clearly left a lasting scar on America and the world. Douglas Brinkley, historian and author at Houston's Rice University, stated that the pandemic was "a seismic event in U.S. history that will be recalled for generations to come."[1] The world will undoubtedly feel the resulting disruption and grief many years from now.

No one in their right mind wants to experience grief, but in this life, it is unavoidable. So, what do we do with the inevitable pain? For some, the tendency may be to overmedicate the hurt, rush through it, or try to ignore it by burying it deep inside. While the unaddressed pain may remain under the surface for a while, it will eventually come out and bring even greater pain in the future. If we do not grieve our losses in healthy and productive ways, we experience what is called "unresolved grief" or, sometimes, "complicated grief." This kind of grief eats at our emotional and relational lives and can leave us perpetually empty and alone to the point where we feel unable to move forward in life. Many people *feel* the pain of their loss, yet because their grief is unresolved, they get stuck in it. Their grieving produces more pain, and rather than diminishing over time, it only worsens. A person with unresolved grief is unable to move forward into a "new normal" and robbed of the abundant life that's described in John 10:10.

Some time ago in a group session for those who had experienced a loss, participants were asked what they hoped they would get out of the meetings. One woman said: "I lost my husband several years ago and don't know how to move forward. It's hardly any different today than it was the week I lost him. I guess I'm stuck and don't know what to do. I want to get unstuck."

Another person responded: "My sister was murdered a few years ago, and I'm very angry with God. I have no peace of mind, and I feel terrible most of the time. I want some relief."

A widower said: "I lost my wife last year, and I feel lost. I'm not sure who I am now. I don't know what to do with all my pain. I *want* to move forward, but how in the world do I do that?"

These people are suffering from unresolved grief. They, like many of us, don't know what to do with their painful feelings. Professional counselors tell us that upwards of 85 percent of all of our struggles to move forward in life after a major loss directly relate to unresolved grief.[2] In other words, if we don't learn to process our grief in a productive way, it can cripple us emotionally and relationally for a long, long time. In and of themselves, grief and suffering don't have value. What brings value and healing out of our suffering and pain is what we do with our grief—how we process it in order to move forward.

What Do I Need to Move Forward?

First, if you are suffering a recent loss, you may not even be interested in moving forward right now. It may feel like it's too early and too painful to even think of that. Because whether you've lost a child, a spouse, a sibling, or dear friend, you'd rather focus on wishing you had the loved one back than on how to move on without him or her. If you've experienced the loss of a dream, health, or hoped-for future, your loss may have such strong ties to that future that it's difficult to imagine any other possible outcome. There is nothing wrong with those feelings. They are to be expected. We cannot turn ourselves around on a dime when our lives have long been intertwined with another person or when we have lost a cherished dream.

So, to one who has just experienced a major loss, the idea of moving forward may feel premature. Or, to those who feel stuck, the effort required to pull oneself out of the mire may feel overwhelming. Grief can be all consuming, especially unresolved grief. The thought of moving forward toward a future that is different from what you had hoped may feel utterly impossible. And the thought of moving forward in life without your loved one may feel unacceptable. You may feel that getting beyond your pain of loss is being disloyal to your loved one.

I felt that way about Austin.

When I lost my sixteen-year-old son, every fiber of my being cried out for him. My motherly instinct wanted to hold my boy and never let him go. To leave Austin's lifeless body and walk out of the hospital that day was one of the hardest things I ever did. Before the casket was closed at the funeral, I ran my fingers through Austin's hair and repeatedly kissed his cheek. I didn't want to leave him. It didn't seem right to imagine life without him. Duane gently held me close and whispered softly, "We are only saying goodbye for now." That may be a good perspective, but it was of little consolation to me at the time.

My dear Austin was gone, and I resisted the thought of him not being with me. It wasn't supposed to be like this. My mind and emotions rejected even the notion of death. I believe in a God who offers eternal life, and the whole idea of death felt so wrong. So placing Austin's lifeless body in a grave and leaving him there wasn't emotionally acceptable. None of our family was really prepared to let Austin go and for him not to be a part of our lives.

We found, however, that on one level, it was not necessary to emotionally let go of Austin in order to move forward and find a new normal. Yes, he was physically gone, and accepting that hard, irrevocable fact took a major adjustment. Yet we found that we could move forward while holding tightly to precious treasures like our love and precious memories of our son. Those who love another person deeply are never required to leave that love behind as they move into the future. The same is true for you. It is not necessary for you ever to let go of the love and memories of the one you have lost. But what each of us needs is to discover how to address any unresolved grief that tries to embed itself in our heart.

At first, our grief simply feels like grief. We don't necessarily label it as unresolved or complicated grief. Our love for the one we lost may, for the moment, be deeply entwined with the grief we are feeling. It's like our pain and our love for that person are wedded together. Subconsciously, we may fear that letting go of any pain caused by our loss and moving forward with lessened grief is paramount to disrespecting the deep love we have for the departed person. Emotionally, it may not seem possible to let go of the grief without letting go of the love. And we surely don't want to let go of that love. So we tend to hold on to both without even realizing it. Our love and all our grief may for a time seem inseparable.

It is proper and healthy to grieve. It is an important part of the healing process. It hurts because there is a hole in our hearts where our loved ones once lived. They are gone, and we miss them terribly. And that hurts. But it is a pure and healthy hurt. The pain of our loss will remain as long as the hole is there. But that doesn't mean our memories of our loved one are forever marred by our loss. In fact, the joy we begin to feel in reliving good memories is an indication that healing is occurring.

Today we have fond and happy memories of Austin. We laugh about his antics and the practical jokes he used to play on us. On some level, he is still part of our family emotionally even though he is not physically present. And the memories, while precious, are still bittersweet because he is not literally with us. Of course, we believe one day we will be reunited with him, and then God "will wipe every tear from [our] eyes, and there will be no more death or sorrow or crying or pain" (Revelation 21:4). But until then, we are able to endure the pain, move forward in life, and establish a new normal without Austin.

The process of grieving in a way that moves us forward can be complex. In this book we will untangle some of that complexity so you can be led to grieve in a productive and healthy way and systematically move forward in your life.

The key question we want to answer for you is this: "How must I grieve in order to move forward?" The good news is this: We, as authors, not only hope to be your guide through this resource, but we also invite you to stop at designated places to encounter Jesus. At these moments, you will have the opportunity to hear and experience Christ's love and care for you. He will be your ultimate Guide through this journey. Let's encounter Jesus now.

ENCOUNTER JESUS

"Yet the Lord longs to be gracious to you;
therefore he will rise up to show you compassion."
Isaiah 30:18 NIV

As you begin your journey through grief, it will help to remember that you're not alone. You're on this journey with a constant companion. He will be present every step of the way.

Imagine that you've come humbly before the throne of grace. You've come to tell the Savior about your journey and about your grief. What would be his response? Isaiah 30:18 reveals the answer: "Yet the Lord longs to be gracious to you; he rises up to show you compassion" (NIV).

Pause quietly to meditate on the Lord. Use your imagination to picture Jesus sitting at the Father's right hand. You approach the Savior and with humility begin to tell him about your grief, loss, and uncertainty. You tell him about your journey and your desire to move forward and experience a new future and hope. With compassion in his eyes, Jesus looks deep into your soul and sees you—really sees you. He rises from the throne of heaven with a heart full of tenderness to embrace you, to comfort you, and to love you. He whispers in your ear: *I'll be with you every step of this journey. You're* not *alone.* Now, let your heart feel the gratitude. Thank Jesus for being with you on this journey.

Jesus, I am grateful when I imagine you rising to show me compassion. I'm especially grateful for...

 L3. A Spirit-empowered disciple experiences God as he really is through deepened intimacy with him.

2

How Long Will This Grief Journey Take?

"This is terrible. It's like my insides are being torn apart."

"I can hardly breathe. I've never felt such gnawing pain."

"I'm in shock. Numb. In disbelief. This all seems surreal."

"I'm emotionally drained. I feel an emptiness, a void, a vacuum, a gaping hole in my soul where he once was. I feel so lost and alone. And I don't think I know who I am anymore."

These are some of the emotions commonly felt by those suffering a major loss. At times it can seem unbearable, and you wonder how long this will last. There is no one-size-fits-all answer. Each individual's recovery from loss is different because each individual is different. There is no set timetable or prescribed stages you must go through before you arrive at a new normal without your loved one. What you experience is uniquely yours because the relationship with the person you lost was uniquely yours. How you respond to your grief will largely determine the length of your journey forward from deep grieving to that new normal. Yet despite these inevitable variations, there are several responses to grief that are common to everyone who suffers loss.

It is not unusual for those grieving to have disrupted sleep patterns. Some people find it hard to sleep after a major loss. Others may stay in bed for days, as if attempting to sleep it all off. Other common responses to a major loss can include feeling numb, a sense of shock, a lack of concentration, a change in eating habits, and depression. Perhaps the most common reaction to loss can be described as your emotional energy riding on a roller coaster. The ups and downs and ins and outs of positive and negative feelings can be exhausting emotionally and physically draining. And you may question whether it will ever end.

Dr. H. Norman Wright, author of *Experiencing Grief*, identifies four indicators that show when a person is successfully moving through the grief process after the loss of a loved one. Those indicators are: (1) a sense of release; (2) renewed sense of energy; (3) ability to make better judgments; and (4) eating and sleeping better. Dr. Wright says, "For many adults it seems to take eighteen to twenty-four months before these four indicators are present."[3]

Does Time Heal All Wounds?

You have probably heard people say, "Time heals all wounds." That isn't true. Time alone does not heal all wounds, but healing does take time. As we've said, there is no set timetable that applies to every situation. But there are certain factors that will determine the time it takes to heal your wounds and recover from your loss.

One factor is in realizing that trying to logically reason your way past your grief will not remedy what you are going through. Most losses make no logical sense. And attempting to rationalize through your grief definitely won't speed up the process. Logic is a function of the brain, and the brain isn't what is wounded. When we encounter a major loss in life, it's not about a broken brain but rather a broken heart. None of us can reason our way through grief to bring healing to the heart.

If you break your arm, you go to the doctor for help. Neither the doctor nor you can reason around the fact that a bone is broken and will need medical attention. There are no quick fixes to a major bone break. It will take time to heal, probably longer than you want. It will require you to patiently endure the process—setting the bone, immobilizing the arm through wearing a cast, and suffering a good bit of discomfort. But by following through on the medical process and taking the prescribed medication, in time, you can heal.

When your heart is broken, you need to give yourself the same freedom for your heart to heal as you would for your body to heal. Accept that you need to follow a process to grieve productively in order to move forward. That process begins by understanding how to move through unresolved grief.

What Hinders Grief Recovery?

Unresolved grief is simply the pain we continue to experience due to a loss that we have not productively processed. The problem is that other factors mix in with our grief and hinder grief recovery.

For example, if someone caused the injury or death of our loved one, we might resent that person and become bitter. The added feelings of resentment and bitterness would complicate the grieving process and keep it unresolved. It's common for grieving people to struggle with "if-only" thoughts. *If only I had done this or that differently, my loved one's death might not have happened.* As a result, needless regrets impede the grieving process. We might blame ourselves in some way and suffer from guilt. We might additionally struggle with anger, fear, and anxious thoughts about the future or even feel a loss of identity since our loved one has passed.

With these and other added elements mingling into our pain of loss, our grieving can become unproductive and remain unresolved. Unless we identify and let go of these added and unproductive elements, they can keep us stuck in a perpetual state of grief.

Imagine your heart with a hole in the center of it representing your loss.

A vacuum will always remain in your heart because your loved one or your dream is gone. That's naturally the case. But the good news is that the pain, as intense as it is, can find an abundant measure of healing if it receives the proper treatment. The purpose of the treatment is to get rid of that unproductive mixture of elements that have trapped your pain within your heart. Only then can you move forward toward healing. The solution is really very simple—just let those contaminating elements go. Of course, simple does not mean easy.

We are grieving because the hole in our heart caused by our loss has left us feeling alone and brokenhearted. The second illustration above shows the hole in the heart surrounded by several contaminating elements that often block healing. Many of these can sneak into our heart unknowingly. Our grief becomes complicated or unresolved when we fail to deal with these unproductive factors. The longer we hold on to them, the longer it will take for us to heal and recover.

Take the time now to stop and reflect on the unproductive elements that might be surrounding your loss. In addition to the grief you feel, what other complications might hinder your healing? Are you experiencing any regret, bitterness, guilt, anger, isolation, struggles with trust, or fear of tomorrow? Write about any of these unproductive elements that come to your mind.

EXPERIENCE SCRIPTURE

Lord my God, I called to you for help, and you healed me.
PSALM 30:2 NIV

Pause and ask God to make this verse true in your life.

Some of the things that might be complicating my grief or hindering my healing include (anger, regrets, aloneness, fear, guilt, struggling to trust, etc.)...

Heal my heart and soul, Lord. I am specifically asking for renewed hope in...

 W9. A Spirit empowered disciple lives "in the present" as God's Word brings healing to hurt, anger, guilt, fear, and condemnation—which are hindrances to an abundant life.

The Incremental Process of Letting Go and Holding On

As we are letting go of those unproductive elements that can creep into our lives, we also need to take hold of some new things. It is actually a process of letting go of the unproductive and holding on to the productive that enables us to move forward to a new normal.

The apostle Paul told us that for him to grow and move forward in his spiritual life, he had to both let go and hold on. He said: "I focus on this one thing: Forgetting [letting go of] the past and looking forward [holding on] to what lies ahead, I press on to reach the end of the race...[And] hold on to the progress we have already made" (Philippians 3:13–14, 16). This same principle applies to how we grow and move forward emotionally through the stages of grief.

When we see that what we are being offered to hold on to is positive and productive, it gives us courage and strength to let go of those things that are holding us back. It is an exciting prospect of letting go in order to move forward. That two-lane road will lead us back to hope-filled thinking and joy-filled living.

The reality is that you have been going through a "letting go and holding on" process your entire life. In fact, at every point in life's journey you have let go of the old in order to hold on to the new. In birth, you let go of the protective and warm embrace of your mother's womb and held on to a process of breathing on your own as a newborn. You let go of nursing in the arms of your mother and held on to the adventure of eating on your own. Eventually you let go of being under the constant care of your mother and father and took hold of thriving on your own. Life is a process of letting go and holding on, and it's not always an easy transition. But that is how we come to experience renewed emotional, relational, and spiritual wholeness and purpose.

When we find our soul mate, we need to let go of our mother and father and hold on to a fresh source of love with the one we marry (Genesis 2:24). We may move from one house to another, trade cars, and purchase new clothes. In all of these transactions, we let go of the old and embrace the new. When we relocate geographically, we leave old friends and find new ones. We leave one community to join yet another. We let go of our children as they become adults (Psalm 127:4). Then we often embrace and hold on to new family connections that may include a son-in-law or daughter-in-law and perhaps grandchildren. Every step forward in life requires letting go and holding on in some fashion. Healing from the pain of grief is no different.

Grieving a loss in a productive way is a process that includes a series of small and repeated choices to let go and hold on. That is what we propose here—making a series of intentional choices to let go of those things that are unproductive and hold on to those things that will help us move forward. We don't need to, nor can we, move through this grieving process quickly or in big chunks. But as you journey with us, it will not just be about choosing to let go and hold on; it will also be about receiving—receiving healing, spiritual strength, a renewed sense of wholeness, peace of mind, and a renewed sense of purpose.

In this journey we will prepare you to repeatedly make choices to:

- **Let go** of the unrealistic expectation that the grieving process will be quick or easy, and **hold on** to the hope that you can move forward to a new normal and a more abundant life.

- **Let go** of certain unproductive views of yourself that lead to grieving alone, and **hold on** to the comfort you receive from others.

- **Let go** of unproductive guilt and regrets, such as wishing you had been there more for your loved one, cared for him better, or shown more love and patience, and **hold on** to the freedom that forgiveness brings.

- **Let go** of unproductive anger you may have, especially toward God, and **hold on** to the belief that he cares and has certain promises for you to claim. You will be able to hold on to the truth that he has a renewed hope and future in store for you.

- **Let go** of anxiety and fears of the future, and **hold on** to the assurance that God is with you and loves you no matter what.

- **Let go** of the unproductive belief that you control your own destiny, and **hold on** to a confident trust that God has your present and eternal future in his hands.

- **Let go** of your past normal by offering God your present broken and shattered life, and **hold on** to your new normal and renewed purpose that God will reveal.

There may be a part of you that thinks, *I'm definitely going to need some help with this process of holding on and letting go. I'll need someone to be my guide.* We can be grateful that we have a Savior who has walked this journey himself. Remember, Christ let go of his exalted place in heaven and held on to his promise to redeem man. He let go of the temptation he experienced in the wilderness and the aloneness he experienced in the garden and held on to the comfort he received from the Father. He let go of any temptation to become angry and bitter toward his accusers and held on to the belief that God's revealed plan for the future would produce ultimate joy (Hebrews 12:2).

Doesn't it strengthen your confidence to know that Jesus has already walked the path you are now treading? Scripture says that Jesus is our teacher. We are his students. The more time we spend with Jesus, the more we'll become like him. "A student is not above the teacher; but everyone, when he has been fully trained, will be like his teacher" (Luke 6:40 NASB).

ENCOUNTER JESUS

"A student is not above the teacher; but everyone, when he has been fully trained, will be like his teacher."
Luke 6:40 NASB

Take a few moments to stop and express your gratitude to this teacher, Jesus. Tell him how you want to be more and more like him.

Jesus, I am grateful that you have been on this journey before me. I'm grateful that you have experienced the challenges of letting go because…

I am grateful you know what it's like and how hard it is to hold on to…

These truths give me hope because…

I want to be more like you in…

L10.   A Spirit-empowered disciple practices the presence of the Lord, yielding to the Spirit's work of Christlikeness.

As we courageously begin to let go—and repeatedly let go—of the things that keep us stuck in our pain, we can miraculously begin to find healing for a broken heart by *holding on to comfort for past losses*. The term *past losses* means other losses in the past that may leave a lingering trail of pain because we have failed to resolve them. We can begin to experience spiritual strength, a renewed sense of wholeness, and emotional peace of mind as we *hold on to God's promises in the present*. And as we continue to choose to let go, we can experience a renewed sense of purpose as we *hold on to God's revealed plan for our future*. (We will discuss God's promises and his revealed plan for your future beginning in Chapter 5.)

Another way to state this progression toward wholeness is, as we learn to process our grief in a productive way, we will be free to take hold of healing comfort from God and others for past losses, claim God's promises to address our present grief, and embrace God's plan for our future healing. This progressive journey in tandem with God will empower us to move forward in life to our new normal.

We are not giving you a rigid prescription or a regimented formula to follow. We are not even suggesting that you make your choices to let go in a certain order of the elements that impede healing. Start with what seems uppermost in your mind, whether it's fear, regret, anger, or some other impediment. The important thing is to keep the process ongoing. Keep repeating your choices until they lead you into your new reality—a new way of thinking and living as you continue to choose to let go of the old and hold on to the new.

Losses come in all kinds of packages. We have mentioned the loss of health or a home, a job, a relationship, and, of course, the loss of a friend or family member through death. Ours was the loss of family health and eventually the loss of our son. Because that is our story, in this book we will often focus on the loss of a loved one through death. However, in the last section we specifically apply the principles of moving from pain to purpose to other types of losses. In that section, we will also make reference to other resources that specifically and more fully address those issues.

If you are currently suffering a loss other than the death of a loved one, we suggest you go to Section Four now. This section covers five common losses. Locate the segment dealing with the loss you are currently experiencing and read through it. There we will help you apply the recovery process to your situation and direct you to applicable information available in the various chapters of this book.

EXPERIENCE SCRIPTURE

For all of God's promises have been fulfilled in Christ with a resounding "Yes!" And through Christ, our "Amen" (which means "Yes") ascends to God for his glory.

2 CORINTHIANS 1:20

Stop now and reflect on the promise of *God's comfort for your past losses* (2 Corinthians 1:3–4). As you are able to hold on to God's comfort, what might healing look like for you? Write about that here:

As you are able to *hold on to God's promises in the present*, what would an experience of spiritual strength, a renewed sense of wholeness, or emotional peace of mind look like for you (2 Peter 1:3–4)? Write about that here:

And as you learn to *hold on to God's revealed plan for your future* what might a renewed sense of purpose look like for you (Jeremiah 29:11)? Write about that here:

Lord, I am claiming that the promises from your Word will be real in my life. I say, "Yes" to your promise of...

 W7. A Spirit-empowered disciple lives the Word through a life explained as one of "experiencing Scripture."

Begin the Letting-Go and Holding-On Process Now

Letting go of the various unproductive elements that may be impeding your healing will require courage, faith, persistence, and patience. You have choices to make. It will take time. So let's get started.

The first letting-go and holding-on choice we suggest you address is:

> *Let go* **of the unrealistic expectation that this grieving process will be quick or easy, and** *hold on* **to the hope that you can move forward to a new normal and a more abundant life.**

This is a small but important choice. Realize that there are no quick or easy solutions to your grief, and then you can make a series of small choices to let go and hold on. You have experienced a major wound to your emotional heart. Your first choice is to accept the reality that your broken heart needs attention and to patiently endure the process of healing. In making this choice, you are holding on to the hope that you can and will move forward. This is a choice you will need to make repeatedly.

One of the first things we did as a couple when Austin was suffering heart failure was to turn to God. If you are a believer in God and trust him for salvation, he is your refuge. God is there for each of us. Choose to trust your situation to God. This will increase your hope for a new tomorrow.

The psalmist David said:

> The Lord is close to all who call on him, yes, to all who call on him in truth. He grants the desires of those who fear him; he hears their cries for help and rescues them. (Psalm 145:18–19)

> God is our refuge and strength, always ready to help in times of trouble. (46:1)

God was a critical part of our healing and recovery. That isn't to say our faith wasn't tested to the limit. It was. We struggled with where God was during the darkest times of our lives. You may struggle with why certain things are happening to you as well. We will get into that area later in this book. Your relationship with God *can* deepen, and you can find true spiritual strength and comfort in him.

God Isn't All We Need

While it is true that we need God above all other things, he designed us to need more than him alone. We need other people in our lives too. We need both God and one another. However, some have latched onto the notion that "All we need is God." One of their favorite verses is: "I can do everything through Christ, who gives me strength" (Philippians 4:13). This would seem to imply that we are spiritually weak if we need anything other than God. Of course, that isn't what the apostle Paul was inferring. In fact, he clarifies this point in the next verse when he says, "Even so, you have done well to share with me in my present difficulty…you sent help more than once" (vv. 14, 16). Paul was making it clear that he was doing everything through Christ, and God was pleased to involve others in that process.

God created us to need him. He wants us to love him, trust in him, and receive from him. But he has also made us in such a way that we need others in our lives. He wants us to love one another, trust in each other, and receive from one another. He created us as relational beings who need both God and one another.

The 2020 coronavirus pandemic may go down in history as the most or one of the most widespread pandemics ever. In an effort to limit the spread of the virus, the nation called for the population to "shelter in place." Government officials told people to stay home, and if and when they needed to go out, they must engage in "social distancing." The set guideline was for people to stay at least six feet apart.

All non-essential businesses had to shut down. People couldn't go to restaurants, bars, gyms, movie theaters—many churches even closed their doors and streamed services online. Schools shut down, and teachers educated their students remotely. Gatherings were limited to only ten people. Parks, beaches, and many walking trails were off limits. And all this took a toll on the nation emotionally. One could say COVID-19 caused a pandemic of human aloneness.

Another tragedy is that those who died due to the coronavirus had to die alone. Hospitals could not allow loved ones of those infected with COVID-19 to be with them due to the infectious nature of the virus. Consequently, people were dying without loved ones by their sides. Healthcare workers did their best and, in many cases, held the hands of strangers in an attempt to ease the pain of dying alone.

Created in the image of a relational God, we all cry out for a relationship with him and with one another. And when that need is not met, we all suffer from human aloneness. The remedy for removing aloneness is simple—close relationships with both God and one another. Scripture reminds us that "we are all parts of his one body, and each of us has different work to do. And since we are all one body in Christ, we belong to each other, and each of us needs all the others" (Romans 12:4–5 NLT*). As relational beings created in God's relational image, he placed within us certain relational needs that he wants us to receive from him and one another.

If there is any time in your life that you need comfort, it's now, while you are suffering from a heavy loss. Yes, God is there to comfort you. He is the ultimate provider and supplier of your needs. But he is pleased to channel some of those provisions through others so that you learn to recognize our mutual dependence and need for one another. "God is our merciful Father and the source of all comfort," Scripture states. "He comforts us in all our troubles so that we can comfort others. When they are troubled, we will be able to give them the same comfort God has given us" (2 Corinthians 1:3–4).

This brings us to another choice in this letting-go and holding-on process:

> **Let go of any notion that you only need God to help you through your loss, and hold on to the truth that you need both God and others on this journey.**

It is unproductive to grieve alone. As Scripture says, "we belong to each other, and each needs all the others" (Romans 12:5 TLB).

Don't Go It Alone

Moving from pain to purpose is a journey you need not take alone. In fact, it is vital that someone walk with you in your grief process. There are specific exercises labeled as "Assignments" in certain sections of this book. After various chapters, you will be encouraged to complete those exercises. We encourage you to invite a friend to interact with you and experience those exercises with you. Invite someone you know well enough to take this journey with you. Your friend will need to read the pertinent chapters so both of you will know how to journey effectively together.

You may be reading this book in order to help a friend who is now suffering a loss. Go to this person and explain that you would like for the two of you to journey together through a process that will take him or her from deep pain to renewed purpose.

Recovering from a deep loss is sometimes complex because we are complex human beings. To help us untangle some of the complexities, we have enlisted the partnership of coauthor Dr. David Ferguson of The Great Commandment Network in Austin, Texas. He has many years of experience in counseling. He also has an in-depth understanding of Scripture. We have enlisted his help in developing the content of this book and the valuable exercises found in the sections entitled "Encounter Jesus," "Experience Scripture," and "Engage in Fellowship."

Dr. Ferguson's message on what constitutes healthy relationships and grief recovery is transformative. We are not only grateful for the message he has poured into this book but also for the personal ministry he and his wife, Teresa, have poured into our lives. Their grief recovery contribution throughout these pages is tried and proven. They have worked to produce healing in our lives and in the lives of countless others. For more information on The Great Commandment Network, please see Appendix 1 in the back of this book.

> **For Small Group Use**
>
> You may be using this book as part of a small group course. Even so, you will still need a partner to engage with in the Experiential and Assignment sections. During group sessions, you will be able to share what you are discovering.

As we travel the country and present our *From Pain 2 Purpose* seminars in churches, we ask people to consistently pray for those going through the grieving process. This means many people are praying for you right now. We are praying for you. Those prayers are specific: *Lord, as those who are suffering from loss go through this process of choosing to "let go and hold on," may you bring healing to their hearts, spiritual strength to their souls, emotional peace of mind, and a renewed sense of emotional wholeness and purpose. Amen.*

ENCOUNTER JESUS

Who then will condemn us? No one—for Christ Jesus died for us and was raised to life for us, and he is sitting in the place of honor at God's right hand, pleading for us.
ROMANS 8:34

Before we begin the full *From Pain 2 Purpose* journey, spend a few moments enjoying more time with the Savior. Let him remind you that he will not only be with you during this journey, he will also be praying for you! How can we know? Scripture tells us that Jesus is in heaven praying for us: "He lives forever to intercede with God on their behalf" (Hebrews 7:25).

Let's make this more personal.

Imagine waking up this morning. The house is quiet; no one else is awake. But you sense that someone else is present. You walk toward the living room where only a small lamp glows in the darkness. Your eyes adjust; you can't quite believe what you are seeing, but there he is. Jesus is on his knees in your living room!

As you walk into the room, you can see his lips moving, and you realize he must be praying. You're careful not to disturb the Savior, so you sit down softly beside him. In the stillness of the morning, you're soon able to make out the words. Suddenly, you realize he is praying for you! It's as if Jesus is sitting beside his heavenly Father, and he is carefully telling him the concerns of your heart. He's praying for your loss and your grief. He's interceding for you as you embark on this journey.

Take some time to join Jesus in prayer. He's praying for you. Why don't you meet him there?

Jesus, I am grateful and amazed that you spend your time praying for me. Thank you that…

Pause and worship the Great High Priest who is praying just for you. Voice your praise for how he intercedes on your behalf.

Let your own journey begin!

 L7. A Spirit-empowered disciple loves the Lord by entering often into Spirit-led praise and worship.

EXPERIENCE SCRIPTURE

The Lord is close to all who call on him, yes, to all who call on him in truth.
He grants the desires of those who fear [respect] him; he hears their cries for
help and rescues them.

PSALM 145:18–19

Take a moment and think about the journey ahead. Write a prayer for God's help and strength in the space below.

Dear Lord, I need you as I make this journey. Help me...

 L3. A Spirit-empowered disciple experiences God as he really is through deepened intimacy with him.

ASSIGNMENT

If you haven't already found a partner to engage with you in this journey, now is the time to invite another person to travel this road alongside you. List the names of three to five people you think would be good options for selecting a journey partner. Be sure to consider your spouse, family members, or close friends among your choices. Prioritize them according to whom you would like to contact first. Pray that God will go before you as you explore which of these people will take this journey with you.

1. _____

2. _____

3. _____

4. _____

5. _____

SECTION ONE

There Is Comfort for You to Receive

3

What a Broken Heart Needs

I (Duane) sat slumped in a chair in a small room just outside the ICU. No one else was in the room. Cindy was getting a bite to eat and trying to get a little rest. My body and emotions were almost at a breaking point. The sleepless nights, the ups and downs of the various treatments for Austin, the emotional stress of trying to stay strong for Cindy, the sense of helplessness—it was all pressing in on me. And the worst was this intense feeling of aloneness. I was suffering emotionally, and I was doing it alone.

Resting the back of my head against the wall, I looked up at the ceiling and prayed out loud, "God, where are you? I need you. I feel so lost and alone. I need someone to talk to. I can't stand this uncertainty."

A volatile mixture of fear, despair, and physical exhaustion overcame me. I began to cry out in heaving sobs. I couldn't control it. "Lord, please help me!" I cried aloud. "Send someone to help me through this."

I was still weeping with my head in my hands when I heard someone come in. I looked up to see a woman looking at me, her face full of tenderness and compassion. She was completely bald. The hospital we were in dealt with many cancer patients, and baldness was commonplace. Yet this woman was not a patient. I later learned that she was a mother whose daughter was at the hospital undergoing chemotherapy. In solidarity with her little girl, she had shaved her own head. Sensing my distress, the woman smiled and said, "Can I give you a hug?" Then she stepped up, wrapped her arms around me, and gave me a gentle hug.

I appreciated the woman's gesture, yet I felt awkward. We spoke for a moment, and then she was called away. I wasn't accustomed to receiving tender touches or comforting words. In fact, I would say I didn't really know how to effectively receive comfort. When I felt painful emotions, my tendency was to talk or pray. So I stepped out of the room to find someone to talk to.

I immediately recognized one of the secretaries of the unit. She greeted me with a smile, but then she saw my face. I must have looked like a wreck. "What's wrong?" she asked, her eyes filled with concern.

"I need to talk to someone," I answered. "Would you call a chaplain, please?"

"Of course!" she replied. She got on the phone immediately, spoke briefly, and then hung up. She smiled and said, "Wait here. A chaplain will be coming up shortly."

I knew that asking to see a chaplain was a little bit risky because you never knew who was on call. In a few minutes the on-call chaplain walked up and greeted me. She was young, no more than twenty-three or twenty-four years old.

We walked back into the waiting room and began talking. I'm not sure what all I was hoping for—perhaps emotional relief of some kind or a spiritual truth to hang on to. But the pep talk or encouraging set of words she recited did little to ease my pain.

What Comfort Is and Isn't

What I needed most and didn't realize it was comfort. That is what everyone who is in emotional pain needs. It's not that words of encouragement or even a pep talk isn't helpful at the right time. But when someone is hurting emotionally, the need of the moment is comfort.

Undoubtedly, your friends and family members meant well with all they have done and said since you suffered your major loss. However, as well meaning as many people are, their comments often appeal more to the intellect than to the heart. If that is the case, those comments, as well intended as they may have been, could have unwittingly invalidated your feelings or provided irrelevant advice. Here are a few examples:

- Loss of a loved one:

  "He led such a full life."

  "She's not suffering now. She's in a better place."

  "I guess it's comforting to know he went quickly and didn't suffer."

  "You can be grateful you were with her as long as you were."

  "It takes time to get over these kinds of things."

- Loss of a dream or divorced:

  "Hope you had good insurance."

  "God will not give you more than you can bear."

  "I bet you're glad the whole ordeal is over."

  "God will give you someone/something even better."

  "Everything happens for a reason."

  "This will make you stronger."

Though the well-meaning people who make these remarks don't realize it, the subtext of their comments is: "Don't feel so bad because you'll soon get through this. And I hope you get over this as soon as possible. I'd like to fix it for you if I could." The implication seems to be that the grieving person should not feel pain too intensely or too long. The problem is that most people haven't learned how to validate the deep pain of grieving people and simply empathize with their suffering.

Most people who know you want to help. They really do. They send cards and flowers. They may bring more casseroles than your refrigerator can hold. Your church may have stepped up and provided a post-funeral reception. If you've lost your home to a disaster, your church and/or neighbors may come to your aid in a major way. These acts are wonderful, needed, and appreciated. But the reality is that many just don't know what to say when faced with your deep, emotional pain.

People who have not experienced deep grief may feel uncomfortable with your grief and just wish you could soon get over it. They may unwittingly apply pressure, saying things like:

"Just wait, you'll see that good will come out of this."

"You're going to make it. God has some great things in store for you."

After hearing too many of such remarks, one grieving person posted on social media: "Am I the only one who feels pressured to turn my grief and loss into some comeback story?…I feel like people want a happy ending and it's on me to produce it."

Then there are those who try to console us by suggesting they know how we feel. "I know exactly how you feel because I, too, lost my (husband/wife, mother/father, son/daughter, etc.)." Or, "I know exactly what you're going through. (I lost my dog last year, or we lost our home to a flood, etc.)."

The truth is that no one except God knows *exactly* how you feel. No two people have the same relationship, and every person attaches to things and people differently. So no person can know exactly what another is going through. Sure, losses can be similar, but it offers little help for a person to compare his losses to those of another who is grieving. Effective empathy and comfort focus on the person who's hurting, not on the one offering comfort. If you are attempting to comfort someone, we encourage you to avoid referring to your experience or what you might have suffered in the past. Being of comfort to another is about focusing on him and sharing in his grief.

A few months after Austin died, a few individuals told us it was time to put our loss behind us. The message was "stop talking about your son and definitely stop getting so emotional." One lady from this group shared this experience: "The morning after my mother's funeral, my father gathered all of us around the table. He told us it was time to move on. There would be no more talk of our mother and no more tears." She suggested we do the same.

These people had good intentions. Yet we felt pressured. But nothing in their attitude or our own hearts motivated us to follow their advice. These "comforters" were much like the three that ministered to Job. They were rather cold and unfeeling and reflected no hint of peace or joy. No doubt the way they had handled their own grief contributed much to the kind of people they had become. As a result, their counsel was of little comfort to us.

What then is true comfort? A word picture for physical comfort might be that of a friend draping a warm blanket over another who is cold or placing a cool, wet washcloth on the brow of one with a high fever. Such efforts attempt to soothe an ailing body and bring physical relief. Emotional comfort is intended to soothe the emotions and bring relief to a broken heart. Pure and simple comfort for the aching heart is a soothing balm to our emotional suffering. Comfort provides solace and eases our grief, it gives immediate relief to the heartache we feel, helps alleviate our emotional pain, and aids in the healing of a broken heart.

It's natural to think that kind of emotional relief would take a good bit of effort on the part of the one offering comfort. How do you come up with the right inspiring words to say, provide sage advice, or offer some profound solution that will alleviate their suffering? All of that might be necessary if we were directing our comfort to the intellect. But emotional comfort isn't intended for the brain; it's for the heart. So what is comfort for the heart? Let's pause a moment and think first about what comfort for the heart isn't.

Comfort for the heart isn't about trying to solve a problem or "fixing" a person who is grieving: "In my opinion, the reason this happened is…"

Comfort for the heart isn't about a pep talk: "I know you're feeling bad now, but in time you'll be much better. How about we go and get something to eat?"

Comfort for the heart isn't about a teachable moment: "There's a reason for everything. In this situation, God instructs us to…"

Comfort for the heart isn't about advice: "I think you're handling things well, but if I were you, I would…"

Again, helping to solve problems, giving pep talks, pointing out teachable moments, and providing advice all have their place. But what a person needs in the moments of pain and suffering is emotional comfort. The grieving person needs the freedom to express the pain he or she is feeling without judgment. One grieving person put it this way: "I'm not allowed to just hurt or have a low season or just hate life because everyone wants the positive."

We offer true comfort without expectation of any certain response from those who are grieving. It's about accepting them wherever they are at the moment and simply being with them, feeling their sadness and pain. You offer true comfort when you experience this biblical passage with your friend: "If they are sad, share their sorrow" (Romans 12:15 TLB). It's about listening to and identifying with the hurt and pain that is being expressed. At times it's about offering the gift of sacred silence and not filling every painful moment with words.

Emotional comfort might look like a warm embrace, a pain-filled face with tears streaming down, or sitting quietly and holding the grieving person's hand.

Emotional comfort might sound like: "I am so sorry you are going through all this." "I can't even imagine the pain you are feeling right now, but I hurt with you." "I want to be with you during this time. Let your pain out, and I'll be here with you. I so hurt with you."

Very few of us have learned to express true comfort to one another. But the reality is that there is such pure simplicity to it. You don't have to provide any answers. There is no pressure to offer a solution or fix anything. You just show up with a caring and compassionate heart and share in your friend's sorrow. It's about being there and feeling the sorrow with him or her. It's essentially a matter of empathizing. The apostle Paul gave us the simplest but most effective way of rendering comfort: "Mourn with those who mourn" (v. 15 NIV). It's mostly a matter of responding to your friend's hurt with real emotion.

The following chart summarizes what comfort is and what it is not.

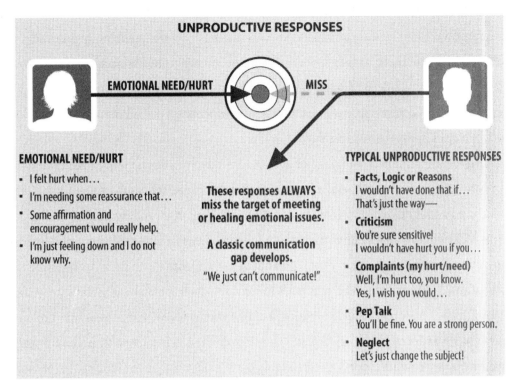

UNPRODUCTIVE RESPONSES

EMOTIONAL NEED/HURT → MISS

EMOTIONAL NEED/HURT

- I felt hurt when…
- I'm needing some reassurance that…
- Some affirmation and encouragement would really help.
- I'm just feeling down and I do not know why.

These responses ALWAYS miss the target of meeting or healing emotional issues.

A classic communication gap develops.

"We just can't communicate!"

TYPICAL UNPRODUCTIVE RESPONSES

- **Facts, Logic or Reasons**
  I wouldn't have done that if…
  That's just the way—
- **Criticism**
  You're sure sensitive!
  I wouldn't have hurt you if you…
- **Complaints (my hurt/need)**
  Well, I'm hurt too, you know.
  Yes, I wish you would…
- **Pep Talk**
  You'll be fine. You are a strong person.
- **Neglect**
  Let's just change the subject!

[Used by permission of the Great Commandment Network © 1994]

Why It May Be Hard to Receive Comfort

Even when we offer the simplicity of pure comfort, it may sometimes be hard for the hurting person to receive it. Some people may have an unproductive or inaccurate view of themselves that hinders their ability to open up to receive comfort. The comfort offered may be heard, but it isn't really received. Therefore, it never reaches deep into the broken heart. This blockage of comfort could result from one of two unproductive views we may have of ourselves—views that we need to let go of.

"I Am Undeserving of Comfort"

Even from the beginning, as a new bride to Duane, I (Cindy) struggled with feelings of inadequacy. Duane seemed to be so accomplished and self-sufficient, and I never felt I quite measured up. Emotionally, I would put myself down. Inwardly, I felt unworthy and struggled with self-condemnation. So when I was suffering through painful losses, I tended to feel unworthy of another person's empathy and compassionate heart of comfort. I didn't consciously think that way, yet somewhere deep inside I didn't feel deserving of another person's time and energy. Even though comfort was offered, my emotional baggage of unworthiness kept it from penetrating my heart.

When we are suffering the pain of a major loss, we need to openly take in and absorb the comfort we are being offered. Healing can't take place without allowing the comfort from God and others to sweep over us and penetrate our hearts. The reality is that each of us is worth being comforted. If you struggle with feelings of unworthiness of comfort, the solution isn't to go through the mental gymnastics of repeatedly telling yourself "I'm worth it; I'm worth it; I'm worth it." The true antidote for a sense of unworthiness is gratefulness.

What I needed to do when someone hugged me, wept with me, or said "I'm so sorry for your loss," was to express a heartfelt "thank you." We don't need to make apologies or excuses for our sorrow. We don't need to feel that we have inconvenienced the person who is offering us comfort. We just need to be grateful that someone is trying to help us.

Make a choice:

> *Let go* **of any sense of unworthiness you might feel, and** *hold on* **to the comfort that is being offered and accept it gratefully.**

It took time, but I began to learn to accept my brokenness along with my imperfections. In fact, I'm still in the learning process. I began to make these words prominent staples in my vocabulary: "Thank you so much"; "I so appreciate your kind words of comfort"; "I am so grateful to you." Continually expressing a heart of gratitude will enable you to hold on to comfort and allow it to penetrate deep into your heart.

"I'm Mature, so I Don't Need the Comfort"

Another obstacle that keeps comfort from bringing healing to a broken heart is a sense that we can handle the suffering and pain on our own.

Growing up, I (Duane) wanted to please my parents and the people around me. I took my responsibilities seriously and wanted to carry my load. To need help from others was paramount to being a burden to them. And I surely didn't want that. This faulty thinking led me to be emotionally self-reliant. I carried this emotional baggage into adulthood and considered neediness to be both emotionally weak and spiritually immature. I wouldn't have stated it that way, but that is the way I viewed my life.

I've come to realize I'm not the only person who has a streak of self-reliance. I've met others who also tend to feel that they're not being strong if they need help from others. If openly expressed, this attitude might sound something like this: "I'm a self-sufficient person who tries to solve my own issues. I don't want to be such a weakling that I can't muscle through this on my own. I just need to be stronger through all this."

This is where the misconception that "we only need God" can lead us to resist accepting comfort from others. We can sometimes falsely equate spiritual maturity with the attitude that *God and I alone can handle this*. I struggled for years with this self-reliant mindset. It left me dealing with my grief alone, and it hindered me from readily applying the healing power of comfort to my broken heart.

This mindset is not easy to overcome. Many like me have spent most of their lives attempting to meet their needs on their own and being strong in themselves. The answer isn't in making a single choice to stop being self-reliant. It's more complicated than that. It will take repeated choices to humbly say no to the temptation to meet your needs on your own. Humility is the antidote to self-reliance. As we cultivate a heart attitude that acknowledges our deep need for God and others, our heart begins to open up to the comfort God is offering through a relationship with him and other people.

If you sense you might be infected with a case of self-reliance, make a choice today that you will begin to:

> *Let go* of the tendency to make it on your own (self-reliance), and
> *hold on* to the comfort that is being offered. Accept it humbly.

Remember, there is a hole in your heart—the empty space that your loved one or your hopes and dreams once occupied. You will always need a measure of comfort when you feel the pangs of that loss. So letting go of any sense of unworthiness or self-reliance will be a repeated choice you will need to make for the rest of your life. And reaching out and holding on to comfort will also be a repeated embrace.

I had to learn through experience that receiving comfort is an ongoing process. At first, I didn't even realize I needed comfort. As in my conversation with the chaplain, I thought I only needed to talk it out.

That day while the chaplain and I were talking, I received two texts, one after the other. They were from two colleagues traveling through town. They wanted to know if it would be okay to stop by and see me. I texted back: "Please come and visit." The conversation ended with the chaplain, and she wished me well.

It wasn't long before my dear friends—who knew our family's situation well—were by my side. They had not coordinated their travel schedule to be with me that night, but the timing couldn't have been better.

These dear colleagues listened as I poured out my frustration and grief. As I look back on it now, I can't remember what they said to me or what they said to God when they prayed aloud for me. What I remember is that they were there, with me, identifying with what I felt, and sharing in the suffering I was experiencing.

I thought I needed to just talk things out with someone. What I really needed was to receive comfort from my friends who deeply cared for me and my family. In time, both Cindy and I began to learn to open up with humble and grateful hearts and let comfort do its healing work. We're still in the learning process.

It's not easy for self-reliant people (or any of us, really) to cultivate a heart of gratefulness and humility. But we must do it because what a broken heart needs most is comfort from God and from others on a continual basis. And the more we develop a grateful and humble heart, the more we can open up and allow comfort to do its healing work.

In the Encounter with Jesus exercise that follows, you will be led to better understand God's heart of comfort. This exercise has helped us and many others to be more receptive and open to the comfort God wants us to receive directly from him. This will help cultivate your heart to be more receptive to others who offer you comfort.

The story of the prodigal son helps us to understand the true heart of God. (Be sure to read Luke 15:11–32.) The most gripping scene in this biblical account pictures the father waiting for his wayward son. He scans the horizon day after day, straining his eyes and hoping to catch a glimpse of his son—the young man who demanded an early inheritance, ran away from home, and squandered every cent his father had so graciously given.

Pause now and receive the Father's acceptance, compassion, and grace. Imagine what it would be like for the Father to welcome you as his "beloved" (Ephesians 1:6 NASB).

1. Like the prodigal, has your own self-reliance ever led you to mistakenly conclude that you could take care of things yourself? Have you ever minimized your need for comfort from God or other people because of a mistaken conclusion that you can handle pain and grief on your own?

2. When the prodigal son returned, broken and penitent, he discounted his own worth to the Father. Have you ever questioned whether you were deserving or worthy of receiving comfort? Have you ever allowed your sense of unworthiness or self-condemnation to rob you of experiencing compassion from the Lord or other people?

3. Which one of these obstacles might at times stand in your way? Write about that here:

Sometimes, it's hard for me to receive comfort because of my self-reliance/sense of unworthiness. I've seen that tendency arise when...

ENCOUNTER JESUS

"While he was still a long way off,
his father saw him coming.
Filled with love and compassion,
he ran to his son,
embraced him and kissed him."
LUKE 15:20

Pause to celebrate this truth: As the Father sees you in the midst of your journey, he is moved with compassion. He longs to show his heart of comfort and the deep compassion he has just for you. You are his beloved!

Receive his compassion and give him thanks.

 L3. A Spirit-empowered disciple experiences God as he really is through deepened intimacy with him.

ASSIGNMENT

What Kind of God Do You See?

You and your journey partner can work through this exercise together, or you can complete it on your own and share it with him or her when you meet.

1. As you think about the major loss you have suffered and how your life has been affected, how do you sense God is feeling toward you right now? You might feel that God has been close to you. You might feel he has been rather distant. Be as transparent as you can as you describe how you sense that God sees you and feels toward you right now. Write it out here.

2. Read the following four passages aloud. You might whisper them quietly to yourself or have your journey partner read them.

   The Lord is merciful and compassionate, slow to get angry and filled with unfailing love. The Lord is good to everyone. He showers compassion on all his creation. (Psalm 145:8–9).

When you [God] open your hand, you satisfy the hunger and thirst of every living thing (v. 16).

The Lord is close to all who call on him, yes, to all who call on him in truth. He grants the desires of those who fear him; he hears their cries for help and rescues them (vv. 18–19).

He [God] heals the brokenhearted and bandages their wounds (147:3).

3. Either you or your journey partner read the following paragraph aloud:

These passages above reflect a God who cares and is compassionate toward you. He doesn't condemn or prod or scold. He is there to comfort you continually and bring healing to your broken heart. The apostle Peter saw this compassionate God in the flesh and said, "Give all your worries and cares to God, for he cares about you" (1 Peter 5:7).

4. Even when we believe God is non-condemning, caring, and compassionate, it is sometimes hard to feel his loving comfort.

- Do you feel God's comfort as much as you would like?

- Do you think you might be holding on to some things that are hindering you from feeling more of his comfort, like a sense of unworthiness or a little self-reliance?

Express to God here in writing (or in prayer) how you would like to feel more of his loving comfort and what you want to let go of that might be a hindrance to receiving comfort from him. Be open and bare your heart to God.

God, I want to feel more of your comfort because...

Please help me let go of...

Sometimes it seems that God is more than we can take in—after all he is the awesome and almighty Creator of everything. Yet he came down to earth and took on human skin in the form of Jesus. While he is still very much God, he relates to us as human beings, and we can relate to him. He suffered and felt the pain of loss. Through actual experience, he understands what you and I feel. Scripture assures us that he "understands our weaknesses, for he faced all of the same testing we do, yet he did not sin. So let us come boldly to the throne of our gracious God. There we will receive his mercy, and we will find grace to help us when we need it most" (Hebrews 4:15–16).

The expression most often used in Scripture to describe how Jesus felt toward those he encountered is that he was "moved with compassion." Whenever Jesus saw people who were blind, crippled, sick, or hungry, he was "moved with compassion." As a result of that compassion, he met people at the point of their need of the moment and brought relief and healing.

This same Jesus is alive and present today in the person of the Holy Spirit. And he can meet your need for comfort just as he did when he walked the earth some two thousand years ago.

In fact, you might remember a story in Scripture of two sisters who lost their brother. Jesus was good friends with this family. When their brother, Lazarus, became very sick, the sisters, Mary and Martha, sent word to Jesus in hopes that he would come and heal him.

Jesus did show up, but Lazarus had already died. Both Mary and Martha shared their disappointment that Jesus didn't show up in time. "Lord, if only you had been here, my brother would not have died" (John 11:32).

Overcome with grief, Mary wept over the loss of her brother. Perhaps it was too late for Jesus to heal Lazarus from his sickness, but it wasn't too late to raise him from the dead. That was what Jesus was about to do. But as Jesus saw his dear friend Mary shedding tears of sorrow, he did something extraordinary. He broke down and wept.

But why? Why would Jesus be crying? He knew that in a few minutes Lazarus would be alive again. So what was he crying for—who was he crying for?

Jesus was moved with compassion, and he was there to meet Mary at the point of her need of the moment. And at that moment, Mary needed comfort. Jesus didn't preach or give her a pep talk or even offer a message on his powers to reverse death. In a few minutes, she would be rejoicing wildly. But at that moment, she needed comfort, and that is exactly what Jesus gave when he wept with her.

This historical Jesus is also the contemporary Jesus. He comes to *you* in the person of the Holy Spirit. Just as he wept for Mary, he also weeps for you. He sees *your* pain. He feels *your* suffering. And his heart hurts with *your* heart.

> Can you envision Jesus actually weeping with you? Express how it makes you feel to know Jesus is still there for you to give comfort at the moment you need it. Write about your responses here and tell your journey partner about these feelings.

ENCOUNTER JESUS

Then Jesus wept.
JOHN 11:35

Now imagine in your mind's eye that Jesus is in the room where you are right now. He reaches out for your hand and speaks to you about your recent loss. He speaks in a gentle, soft voice. *Read aloud what he is saying:*

I have watched as you have shed tears of sorrow, and I have wept too. My heart is moved with compassion because of your grief.

Your loss grieves your heart as well as mine. Your pain is deep and real, and I am saddened by it.

Your loved one is gone, and you cannot hear that sweet voice or know that loving touch on this earth ever again. In this present life, you cannot show love to your lost one or receive it in return. And oh, how that hurts you! And it hurts me too!

Will you allow me by my Spirit to wrap my arms around you right now? I would like to hold you, weep with you.

I want you to feel that I am here for you. I want to help fill the void in your heart. For I will never leave you. Will you allow me to share in your suffering in that way and bring a measure of comfort to your broken heart?

Now it's time for you to respond with gratitude to the invitation of the comforting Jesus. Put your response in writing.

Jesus, as I reflect on your sorrow for my great loss, my heart is moved with…

 W1. A Spirit-empowered disciple is frequently led by the Spirit into deeper love for the One who wrote the Word.

If you have not had your journey partner with you as you went through this Experiential, then walk carefully through it with him or her when you get together. Read this Experiential aloud and share your responses. Be sure to include your reflections on these promises from God's Word.

> "Do not be afraid or discouraged, for the Lord will personally
> go ahead of you. He will be with you; he will neither fail you nor
> abandon you." (Deuteronomy 31:8)

> "And be sure of this: I [Jesus] am with you always, even to the end
> of the age." (Matthew 28:20)

4

A Backlog of Hurts

"Come on, Charlie, let's go to the woods." When I (Duane) was a boy growing up, those words would bring my faithful dog running to me, and we'd be off for another adventure. Charlie was my childhood companion. Whenever I was outside, my dog was there with me.

One day I went out and called to Charlie, but he didn't come. I looked everywhere for him. I called him until my voice was hoarse, but no Charlie. My dog had suddenly disappeared without a trace, and I never saw him again. I was devastated. My father tried to console me by saying, "It will be all right. I'll get you another dog."

I really didn't want another dog. I simply wanted Charlie back. My dad did get me another dog, and in time I connected with my new pet. But as I look back on it, I really wasn't guided in how to deal with my loss in a productive way.

Our lives are made up of a continuum of experiences from happy moments to painful moments and everything in between. We are people with hopes and dreams who enjoy life's blessings and endure life's difficulties. We have no problem enjoying the good things in life. It's the painful experiences we would like to avoid. Yet painful experiences are a part of life. And how we deal with those hurtful moments in our lives, starting from childhood, largely shapes who we are today. How we deal with hurts also greatly influences how we navigate through life—how we respond, react, and relate to people and to situations.

The truth is that few of us have learned from childhood how to work through our painful experiences, receive loving comfort, and find healing for those emotional hurts. That leaves us with unresolved hurts. If we haven't addressed those past hurts, that unresolved pain builds up a backlog of suffering in our lives. While those unresolved painful experiences are in our past, they can still affect us negatively. In fact, the major pains from our past can radiate into our present and complicate the healing process for our current loss.

No one taught me how to be transparent, to share my pain openly with others, or to receive comfort. Consequently, I wasn't prepared to deal with the painful experiences that would confront me in adulthood. You may not have been taught how to deal effectively with painful experiences either. I won't burden you with all the details, but allow me to share a few major touchpoints of my painful experiences to illustrate how they can compound one upon the other to ripple into our present life. Following is a chart identifying at what age I experienced various events, both happy and painful.

AGE	LIFE EXPERIENCES
25	Married Cindy. Happy time.
27	Son Austin born with heart defect and at 8 months had a heart transplant. Painful time.
29	Daughter Brianna born healthy. Happy time.
32	Daughter Alisha born with heart defect and at 3 months had a heart transplant. Painful time.
33	At age 6 Austin is diagnosed with lymphatic cancer and undergoes 6 months of chemotherapy. Cancer goes into remission. Painful time.
34	At age 7 Austin's cancer reemerges. Extensive surgery and more specialized treatments. Painful time.
36	3-year-old Alisha goes into anaphylactic shock and almost dies. Painful time.
37	At age 4 Alisha has allergies with skin issues so bad she is unable to walk. Painful time.
38	10-year-old Austin faces several heart rejection issues and will need another heart transplant. Painful time.
41	13-year-old Austin is diagnosed with coronary heart disease. Painful time.
43	15-year-old Austin undergoes another heart transplant. Painful time.
44	16-year-old Austin dies of post-transplant complications. Painful time.

For seventeen years of my married life, I had to stand by and watch my son and daughter go through unimaginable pain and suffering while I was helpless to stop it. If it had been Cindy or I who was physically suffering, it would have been different. As adults we could have at least understood what was going on. But little children! That is what hurt me the most.

My innocent son and daughter were hurting, and I could do little about it. When they looked at me, even when they were too young to speak, it felt as if they were trying to say, "Daddy, please help me! Take me away from here and make the pain go away."

Then after all the years of pain and suffering, after the terrible roller-coaster ride of emotions, Austin died. A part of each of us as a family died the day we lost him. It was like a piece of us was buried with him. It was horrific.

Yet, if Cindy and I had not begun to deal with the seventeen years of painful moments one experience at a time, I don't know where we would have ended up emotionally. We could have become a couple of very bitter and angry people who resented God and hated life. I don't really know where we would have been, but I don't think it would have been a good place spiritually, emotionally, or relationally.

What I do know is that not allowing our painful experiences to build up inside has enabled us to better hold on to comfort for each instance of hurt—to absorb it and emotionally begin to move forward in life. Ignoring our pain by just not dealing with it compounds the hurts until it begins to affect us in a myriad of unproductive ways.

In other words, unresolved pain in our past will complicate the recovery of our present major loss. Removing the complication of unresolved pain is simple but not necessarily easy. It is a matter of delving into the past, identifying major painful events over the timeline of our lives, and taking hold of healing comfort for each hurt individually.

To some that might seem scary. Many feel understandably apprehensive about probing the past that has been hidden so long. Their thinking might be, *The past is in the past, and it's best to leave it there.* The problem is that past unresolved hurt is not left in the past. We carry it with us like baggage into our present. When we bury our emotional hurt, we bury it alive. And it will invariably come out in some form that is unhealthy.

According to the National Institute of Mental Health of Bethesda, Maryland, when we experience major painful experiences, especially in childhood, our brain stores the memories, often deep within our subconscious. But because the experience has not been resolved, it will eventually express itself in various symptoms. Those symptoms can include bad dreams, frightening thoughts, feeling tense or on edge, sleeping difficulties, angry outbursts, negative thoughts about oneself, avoiding contact with people, and secluding oneself.[4]

Other pain specialists further confirm the findings that unresolved emotional pain can affect us physically: "When you are continually exposed to emotional pain, there are changes in the brain that produce a dependency on those feelings. And while this emotional pain can be significant and debilitating, when it continues on for a prolonged period of time, it also can end up affecting your physical health as well."[5]

Count on it. Any unresolved emotional hurts in our past are equally in our present. And they will remain there until we courageously face them and begin to find healing comfort for them. But as we said, that prospect can seem scary. We may fear the process of uncovering past hurts. And that brings us to another letting-go choice. We encourage you to:

> *Let go* **of the fear of addressing past hurts. Openly identify them,**
> **share them, grieve them, and** *hold on* **to the comfort given by God**
> **and your friend that brings healing to each past hurt.**

When you stop to think about it, it is really rather simple. We get hurt emotionally; we allow ourselves to feel it and grieve it; we receive caring comfort from another; we find healing, and we continue to move forward with life. Jesus expressed it simply and clearly: "God blesses those who mourn, for they will be comforted" (Matthew 5:4). The good news is that if we weren't taught how to respond to grief when we were young, we can have a do-over as adults.

We can bring to the surface unresolved hurts from the past and receive comfort for them. The process will involve holding on to comfort and applying it to our past wounds. In fact, we will need a continuing source of comfort for the rest of our lives. It is an ongoing process as life inevitably brings new hurts. Over time as we remember painful memories and receive healing comfort, it will clear the way to find a deeper and more lasting healing for the pain of our present loss..

Your next assignment is to create your own personal Chart of Past Hurts. The exercise is designed to help you walk through your past hurts and find comfort for any unresolved emotional pain.

ASSIGNMENT

A Chart of Past Hurts

You should complete this assignment prior to meeting with your journey partner. Then you will share your chart with him or her.

In this chart, you will highlight the major losses you have experienced over your lifetime. In listing your losses, include not only the worst, such as deaths and illnesses but also list other major changes, such as your first romantic breakup or a time you had to move away from friends. Any significant change can result in a painful loss.

Your chart will begin at birth. Enter your earliest memory of a loss of any kind. From that point, continue to identify each subsequent major loss and list your age at the time you experienced it. List the ones you feel were most significant to you. Your list may cover anywhere from ten to fifteen past major losses.

Your earliest memory of a loss may be at around five or six years old. The next may be at eight or nine years. Note your age and identify your losses using short statements like "Broke up with my first 'love,'" "Was bullied," "Moved away," "Sexually abused," "Parents divorced," "Experienced emotional or physical abuse," or "Death of loved one."

Approximate Age	Loss Identified
3-5	_____
_____	_____
_____	_____
_____	_____
_____	_____
_____	_____
_____	_____
_____	_____
_____	_____
_____	_____
_____	_____
_____	_____
_____	_____
_____	_____
_____	_____
_____	_____
_____	_____

After listing your major past hurts, the next step is to rate the intensity level of each based on how you sense it impacts you today. Use an intensity scale of 1–10. On your chart, rate each event according to the intensity you feel it today. For example, your first romantic breakup would probably have rated a 10 when it occurred. Yet today may feel more like a 3.

The idea is to identify how your past hurts still radiate and impact you today. To help you create your own chart, we have created the following sample chart as a model to guide you.

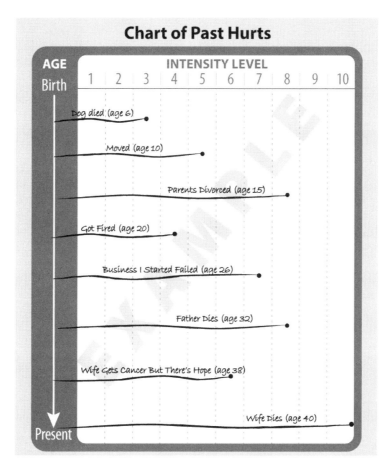

At first, creating your Chart of Past Hurts may not come easy. Yet it will be helpful for you to do it. Don't over analyze the process or try to list all the losses you can remember. Simply record the most significant ones up to the present. When you have completed your chart, you are ready to meet with your journey partner.

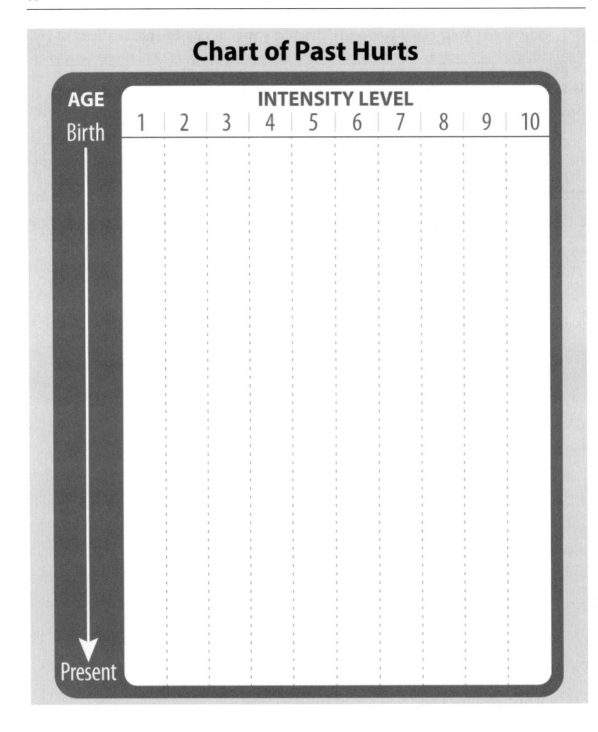

Meeting Time with Your Journey Partner

Note to Your Journey Partner

Your grieving friend has completed a Chart of Past Hurts. That is quite an accomplishment. Praise is in order! Going through the process of charting a history of losses can be emotionally exhausting. Celebrate your friend's courage and diligence to complete it.

As your friend shares these various past hurts, be there to listen and feel the pain with him or her. This isn't a time to analyze or reason why certain things happened. You are not a fixer or advisor at this point. You are a comforter. Share in the sadness of those past hurts with your dear friend.

Years of losses have accumulated, and it can be a little overwhelming to your friend to sense just how much loss and suffering has occurred. Be a conduit of God's loving comfort. Invite God into the room. As you wrap your comforting arms around your friend, know that your arms are joined by the comforting Jesus. If tears fill your eyes and spill onto your cheek, know they are mingled with the tears of Jesus for your friend. Through the power of the Holy Spirit, Jesus' presence is in the room. The great Comforter is bringing healing to a broken heart (2 Corinthians 1:3–4).

Once the charted past hurts are identified, grieved, and comforted, focus on your friend's present major loss. Completing this exercise doesn't mean every past hurt is fully healed. But the process has begun, and you and your partner are ready to address the present loss. Realize that God again is involving you in his ministry of comfort as you become a conduit of the "Father and the source of all comfort. He comforts [you] in all [your] troubles so that [you] can comfort others" (vv. 3–4). Both you and your grieving friend can claim the promise that "God blesses those who mourn, for they will be comforted" (Matthew 5:4).

ENCOUNTER JESUS

Before meeting with their grieving friend, many partners find it helpful to have a fresh reminder of God's comfort for themselves. So take a moment to remember a time when *you* experienced loss, sadness, or grief of some of kind. It could have been the death of a family member, a health or work challenge, a relationship that was disrupted, or any other significant loss. Remember that time and then carefully consider this: *During my moments of grief, what was Jesus feeling for me? What was his heart's response as he saw my pain and my struggle?*

Scripture is clear and consistent about the answer. Jesus wept for his friend Mary who was grieving over the loss of her brother (John 11:35). Jesus was moved with compassion for the man who had lost his health, his community, and his family to leprosy (Mark 1:41). The amazing truth is that the Savior's heart feels the same emotions for you. Because he is the same yesterday, today, and forever (Hebrews 13:8), your grief saddens his heart today just as theirs did over twenty centuries ago.

Take some time now to thank God for his compassion. Imagine his words of compassion for your time of loss. Praise him for his goodness toward you.

God, when I imagine the truth that you feel sadness and compassion for my grief, I am thankful that...

 L1. A Spirit-empowered disciple practices thanksgiving in all things.

ENGAGE IN FELLOWSHIP

All praise to God, the Father of our Lord Jesus Christ. God is our merciful Father and the source of all comfort. He comforts us in all our troubles so that we can comfort others. When they are troubled, we will be able to give them the same comfort God has given us.

2 CORINTHIANS 1:34

After you have expressed your gratitude to the Lord for his comfort, you are ready to share this same comfort with your partner. God has comforted you so that you can comfort others (vv. 3–4).

As your partner begins to share his or her account of loss and grief with you, be sure to consider the same questions as above. What do you feel *for* your partner? How does it move your heart with compassion to hear your friend's grieving words? Here are some helpful and appropriate things you can say in response:

- *It makes me sad to hear you say…*

- *I feel compassion for you about…*

- *My heart hurts to know that…*

- *I am just so sorry that…*

- *I care for you, and I'm committed to going through this with you.*

Pray together. Continue to be an ongoing source of comfort to your friend. Thank God that a broken heart is in the process of healing.

 P3. A Spirit-empowered disciple discerns the relational needs of others with a heart to give of his love.

SECTION TWO

There Are Promises for You to Claim

5

"God, Don't You Care?"

"Mommy, my head hurts," six-year-old Austin said to me (Cindy) as he tugged on my skirt.

"Where exactly does it hurt?" I asked.

Little Austin put both hands on his head. "It hurts here, Mommy."

I gave him some Motrin. When that didn't help, I scheduled an appointment with the pediatrician. The doctor suspected an ear infection and prescribed an antibiotic and more pain medication. But nothing seemed to help.

Eventually, Austin was in so much pain he couldn't even sleep. He repeatedly told me of his pain, and then one morning he said, "Mommy, why don't you care that my head hurts so bad?"

At that point I could hardly take it anymore. I pulled my son close and told him I did care, but I didn't know what more I could do. I cried out to God with the same question my son was asking me, "God, don't you see what's happening? Don't you care that Austin is suffering? Why don't you do something about it?" Yet, at that point heaven seemed closed off by a wall of brass. I couldn't hear or feel anything from God. He seemed silent.

Austin worsened, so we took him to an ear, nose, and throat specialist. Finding nothing in Austin's ears that should cause such intense pain, the specialist ordered an X-ray of his head. A full body scan was eventually ordered. We weren't prepared for the results. Cancer had spread throughout Austin's body, especially in his kidney area. A biopsy identified his cancer as a lymphoma of a particularly aggressive kind that doubled in size every twenty-four hours. Austin, as a heart transplant patient, was immune suppressed. Therefore, the lymphoma was spreading rampantly throughout his body. The oncologist was blunt. "It's not good news," he said. "Unless your son responds very quickly and favorably to the chemotherapy, he only has about two weeks to live."

I have been a Christian since childhood. I knew in my head that God was good, and he cared. But I confess there were times I just felt that he had abandoned me personally and us as a family. I remember at one point praying, *God I want to believe that you are good. I don't feel it right now, but I'm choosing to believe you are good and you do care.* Holding on to that belief in my heart, I tried to keep it together when people were around.

There were times when people who knew what we were going through would try to be of encouragement, saying something like, "I just want you to know that God has been using your children and your situation to challenge and encourage me. You've been a blessing to us." I'll have to say that did little to comfort me. The real problem was that the whole situation was beginning to taint my view of God. He was not intervening on behalf of my sick children, and I was on the verge of becoming bitter.

At one point after someone commented about our children being a blessing to them, I said to Duane, "If that's true, then I think God has used our children enough to bless others. He needs to start using some other children for that. He's used ours enough!"

Blinded to His Goodness

Your tragic loss may seem senseless just as ours did to us. I (Duane) tried to console Cindy and encourage her to stay strong spiritually. Yet it's difficult to be spiritually strong when your loss seems so senseless and you're beginning to question God. Why doesn't God stop all the suffering? And why would he even allow it in the first place?

Theologians tell us that God never wanted humans to experience suffering and death. Yet, if love was to be authentic and real, he needed to create humans with a free will. I guess it makes sense on one level that a person can't be forced to love; it must be expressed freely and voluntarily.

Biblical scholars say that God could have programmed the first humans to automatically be other-focused and always put him and each other first. But a robotic or forced "love" is not real love, and it would not give anyone a true sense of satisfaction or enable a meaningful relationship.

For humans to enjoy the meaning of real love, their choice had to be real. They had to be free to choose either good or evil, to love or not to love. And for that choice to be real, it had to come with the possibility of both positive consequences for right choices and negative consequences for wrong choices. The negative consequence of separation from God was the natural result of humanity's wrong choice. And with separation from a life-giving, good, and perfect God comes all kinds of suffering, heartache, and eventual physical death.

While that explanation is true and makes perfect and logical sense, it doesn't change the reality that death and suffering goes against every fiber of our being. I believe we emotionally reject death because from the very beginning, God designed us to be immortal. Death was never God's intention for us. Wise Solomon knew this when he said, "God has made everything beautiful for its own time. He has planted eternity in the human heart" (Ecclesiastes 3:11).

God had to allow suffering and death because he had to honor the first humans' free choice, even when they chose evil over good. But he was deeply grieved at the chain reaction of suffering that brought the evil consequences of their sin down through the centuries and into our present time. That is why in the very day of that first sin, God announced his ultimate solution. He would come down to the world, experience our griefs and pains himself, and ultimately die to give us a path back to him (2 Corinthians 5:21; 1 Corinthians 15:21–23).

That loving heart of God grieving at our pain is what Cindy and I were not seeing while in the depths of our despair. We were not seeing the true character of God. But when we began to get a glimpse of God's heart on this issue, it radically changed our attitude toward God and our suffering.

After Austin's second round of chemotherapy, I drove him back to the house. I helped him out of the car, gathered the belongings, and headed for the front steps.

"Come on, son," I said as I began to climb the steps.

"I'm coming," he responded.

As Austin began climbing the steps, his legs grew weary. Overwhelmed with weakness, he fell to his knees and began to crawl, one step at a time.

I looked back to see my son laboring for every breath. He looked up at me and said, in almost a whisper, "Daddy, I can't make it anymore. Can you carry me?"

At that moment, an overwhelming feeling of hopelessness flooded over me. Sure, I could pick up my son, but I couldn't change the horrible thing that was happening to him. Cancer racked my son's body, and I was helpless to cure him.

I cried out to God, "Please do something for my son. And if you won't, please give us strength to go through this. Will you please carry each of us?"

Growing up in a Christian home, I learned that God loved us, that he was all-powerful, and that miracles were possible. I knew in my head that I had to continue to trust in God. I could quote from memory Proverbs 3:5–6: "Trust in the Lord with all your heart; do not depend on your own understanding. Seek his will in all you do, and he will show you which path to take."

But at this point in our lives, neither Cindy nor I could see any good path to take. In our heads and hearts, we wanted to hold on to the belief that God was good. Scripture told us that:

> The Lord is good and does what is right. (Psalm 25:8)

> The Lord is righteous in everything he does; he is filled with kindness. (145:17)

> Give thanks to the Lord, for he is good! His faithful love endures forever. (136:1)

But I admit, at times all the pain and suffering our children were going through seemed to override my thoughts about a good God. I tended to question him and wonder where he was during our darkest days.

I wasn't seeing clearly. My pain and anger blinded me and kept me from seeing God's true heart of goodness and care. God saw my struggles and made me some very important promises, but my pain held my focus so fully that I failed to truly trust God and claim the promises that he made to his children.

He Truly Hurts When We Hurt

I wasn't the first to be so preoccupied with my pain and suffering that I didn't see God correctly. The righteous man Job faced such a succession of horrible tragedies that he cursed the day he was born. He asked, "Why is life given to those with no future, those God has surrounded with difficulties?…I have no peace, no quietness. I have no rest; only trouble comes" (Job 3:23, 26).

From a position of pain, King David asked anguished questions of God. His life was turned upside down, and God seemed distant and silent.

> O Lord, how long will you forget me? Forever? How long will you look
> the other way? How long must I struggle with anguish in my soul,
> with sorrow in my heart every day?…Turn and answer me, O Lord my
> God! (Psalm 13:1–3)

David was suffering, and he couldn't understand where God was when he needed him so desperately. It all seemed so unfair. Our loved one has been taken from us. We may be loaded down with added responsibilities or left with debts or helplessly watching the suffering of our innocent children. Where is God in all of this? Does he even care about this senseless suffering we must endure?

The Journey from "Asking Why" to "Does He Care?"

When studying the Bible we find few emotionally satisfying answers as to why God allows suffering and doesn't immediately stop it. But we can gain an insight into how God feels about it. Granted, when we are suffering, it's difficult for any of us to take notice of what God is feeling when we are deep in the throes of pain. But when we do reach the point where we understand his heart, it changes everything.

Notice God's reaction when his chosen people turned from him and suffered the negative consequences of their rebellion. "When Israel was a child," God said, "I loved him, and I called my son out of Egypt. But the more I called to him, the farther he moved from me… Oh, how can I give you up, Israel? How can I let you go?…My heart is torn within me, and my compassion overflows" (Hosea 11:1–2, 8). Hosea the prophet reminds us: God cares!

That is God's response even when we suffer the consequences of our own sin and failures. When God saw all the wickedness in Noah's day, Scripture says, "It broke his heart" (Genesis 6:6). How much more does his heart tear when our suffering is not of our own doing and is so unfair and unjustified? He weeps with us, and as King David said, he is a compassionate God who "gives righteousness and justice to all who are treated unfairly… The Lord is compassionate and merciful, slow to get angry and filled with unfailing love" (Psalm 103:6, 8). The psalmist reminds us: God cares!

That compassionate response from God comes out of his righteous, holy, and good heart. He is "the one who is holy and true" (Revelation 3:7). "He is a faithful God who does no wrong; how just and upright he is!" (Deuteronomy 32:4). It is out of this holy, good, and loving heart that he cares and is heartbroken that we suffer.

As I began to shift my focus toward the heart of God, I began to see that he was compassionate toward me. And that tenderized my own heart. The more we can see God's tender and compassionate heart toward us, the more we can know he truly loves and cares for us. And out of that love, he has promised to be there for us—to strengthen and help us. "God is our refuge and strength, an ever-present help in trouble" (Psalm 46:1 NIV).

Cindy and I had a choice to make. We could hold on to our anger and keep asking, Why God?, or we could refocus on the heart of God and his care for us. We could believe he cares, even when that includes suffering as part of our lives. We could believe he was good even though we didn't have the answers as to why we were suffering. And that is what we did. We made an ongoing let-go-and-hold-on choice—a choice we are continuing to make. It is an ongoing choice that we encourage you to make as well.

> **Let go of any anger and questioning as to why God has allowed your suffering. Hold on to the belief that he cares and claim his promises as your own.**

Reach out in faith, continue to claim these promises as yours, and hold on to them.

> You light a lamp for me. The Lord, my God, lights up my darkness…God's way is perfect. All the Lord's promises prove true. He is my shield for all who look to him for protection. (Psalm 18:28, 30)

> For the Lord is good. His unfailing love continues forever, and his faithfulness continues to each generation. (100:5)

> I will be glad and rejoice in your unfailing love, for you have seen my troubles, and you care about the anguish of my soul. (31:7)

> The Lord always keeps his promises; he is gracious in all he does. The Lord helps the fallen and lifts those bent beneath their loads… The Lord is close to all who call on him, yes, to all who call on him in truth. He grants the desires of those who fear him; he hears their cries for help and rescues them. (145:13–14, 18–19)

Continue to make the promises of God personal through this encounter with Jesus.

ENCOUNTER JESUS

Now hope does not disappoint,
because the love of God has been poured out in our hearts
by the Holy Spirit who was given to us.
ROMANS 5:5 NKJV

Set aside time with your journey partner to celebrate God's special care as he gives us his Spirit.

God doesn't just relate to us as a Father who looks down on us from heaven or even as a compassionate friend who walks among us as Jesus did. If we have accepted God's gift of salvation, God lives within us as part of our very being. By the Holy Spirit, he is not only with us; he is also in us and is thus available to us anywhere at any time.

Here are just some of the blessings that are available to you because of your relationship with Jesus, because his Spirit lives inside you, and because you have received God's gift of salvation. We can celebrate that Jesus says:

- I will never leave you alone (Matthew 28:20).

- I will be your helper and your Counselor (John 14:16; 16:7).

- I will guide you when you need to know the truth (16:13).

- I will strengthen you (Philippians 4:13).

- My Spirit will reveal the things of God to you (1 Corinthians 2:10).

- My Spirit can help you in your weaknesses (Romans 8:26).

- My Spirit intercedes for you; he prays for you (v. 26).

Which of these blessings gives you the most hope at this time?

As I consider the promises that are available to me through my relationship with Jesus, I am most glad to know...

God, thank you for your promises. It's these promises that give me hope to...

 L10. A Spirit-empowered disciple practices the presence of the Lord, yielding to the Spirit's work of Christlikeness.

Finding Increased Spiritual Strength

We began to claim God's promises that he is good and loving and that he will be with us, comfort us, and strengthen us even as we struggled understanding why we were having to endure such suffering. And in little, incremental ways, we began to see that "the Lord is a shelter for the oppressed, a refuge in times of trouble" (Psalm 9:9). I (Cindy) can't count the number of times God revealed his presence to us, giving us that needed refuge and inner strength.

The chemotherapy Austin went through for the cancer became almost unbearable. The pain was especially intense in his stomach and intestinal area. The morphine pump that administered doses every five minutes took off the sharp edge, but little Austin still was in deep pain.

Duane and I often sat beside him, put our hands on his stomach, and rubbed his mid-section gently until he fell fitfully into sleep. I remember praying and claiming God's promise to be with us. Even though Austin was suffering so, I wanted him to sense God cared and had not abandoned us. Of course, I had no idea how well a six-year-old could comprehend the idea of God being with us in our suffering. But I prayed very specifically that God would confirm to me that he was there with Austin.

About a week later Austin said, "Mommy, last night after you left, my tummy was really hurting."

"I'm sorry I had to go, honey," I said. "I just had to get some rest."

"No, that's okay," Austin replied. "Someone else helped me anyway, and I don't know who it was—maybe Jesus."

"What do you mean? What happened?"

"Well, my tummy really started hurting again, and I felt someone rubbing it. And when I looked around, I didn't see you or Daddy or anybody. But somebody I couldn't see was rubbing my tummy. And all the pain went away, and I went right to sleep."

As I listened to Austin, I began to cry. I realized God was letting my son know that he cared and was with him and with us as a family. It began to dawn on me that Jesus was with me all along, even as I was struggling to trust in him and claim his promises. He was with me; he was with Austin; he understood what we were going through, and he cared.

In fact, it seemed God was trying to get our attention to let us know that he had been with us from the very beginning of our journey of suffering. I began to realize that his care had begun on that day we called 911 after our five-month-old Austin stopped breathing. Duane was trying to perform CPR on Austin at the gas station just as the ambulance arrived to rush our baby to the hospital. I related earlier that a female paramedic had jumped into the ambulance with us, and when the male medic froze up and seemed unable to work on Austin, she took charge and began treating him.

When we arrived at the hospital, the medical staff rushed Austin into the emergency room. As I stood back to allow them space, I thanked the paramedic lady who had saved Austin and asked for her name. I wrote her name down and then quickly made my way into the ER.

Days later, I made a trip to the ER to thank this woman for saving Austin's life. I had her name and asked for her specifically. But all I got was blank stares from the staff. No one there knew anyone by that name. It was as if this lady had never existed. Then it dawned on me—perhaps God was sending a message. Was this mystery woman a guardian angel sent to remind me that God was really with us and had been from the beginning?

This was the first of many reminders that "the Lord helps the fallen and lifts those bent beneath their loads" (Psalm 145:14). He is there for you too. He not only feels your pain, but he is also there to lift your load and give you strength.

> The Lord is my strength and shield. I trust him with all my heart.
> (Psalm 28:7)

> O my Strength, to you I sing praises, for you, O God, are my refuge.
> (59:17)

> The Lord says, "I will rescue those who love me. I will protect those
> who trust in my name. When they call on me, I will answer; I will
> be with them in trouble. I will rescue and honor them. (91:14–15)

Take a moment and thank God for being there for you. He may still *feel* distant, but the reality is that he is with you, and he wants to assure you that despite your pain and suffering, he cares about what you are going through. Here is our prayer for you.

Lord, we know you hurt for our friends who are now reading this book. You want them to feel your presence. Help them right now to let go of any anger and their questioning of why. Let them reach out and hold on to a firm belief that you are good and that you have a tender heart toward them. Help them to continue to trust in you even when they don't understand. Strengthen their faith. Make your loving presence known to them. We know you love them so very much. Amen.

ASSIGNMENT

"Can You Hear Me Now?"

You and your journey partner can work through this exercise together, or you can complete it on your own and share it with him or her when you meet together.

From 2002 to 2011, Verizon aired a commercial featuring the "Test Man" in his Verizon jacket and horn-rimmed glasses stepping across the screen holding his cellphone to his ear. He stopped and asked, "Can you hear me now?" Then he stepped forward again, stopped, and repeated the question. He was promoting good phone reception. Wireless reception was as important back then as it is today.

The same is true of our spiritual reception. It's important that we hear clearly what God is saying to us.

There are times when it may seem more difficult to hear clearly from God after a major loss. Write a personal prayer to God telling him about your desire to hear him.

Jesus referred to himself as the "Good Shepherd" and those who follow him as his "sheep." He said, "My sheep listen to My voice, and I know them, and they follow Me" (John 20:27 NASB). Following Jesus is predicated on hearing his voice clearly.

Throughout human history, God has spoken to his children. One night God called out to a young child named Samuel. He thought his guardian, Eli the priest, was calling him. Eli told Samuel that if he heard his name called again, he should answer in a certain way. The Lord called to him again, and Samuel responded as he was directed, "Speak, your servant is listening" (1 Samuel 3:10).

Even in our pain, we are called to hear God's voice and listen to him. That is how our faith is strengthened. Today God largely speaks through his Word. "Faith comes from hearing the message," Paul writes, "and the message is heard through the word about Christ" (Romans 10:17 NIV).

So far in your grief journey, what message from the Word of God has been particularly relevant to your situation? What relevant truth or message have you heard most prominently? Write it out here.

God's Word provides us with numerous promises. The promise to remake us in Christ's image is especially significant. "For God knew his people in advance, and he chose them to become like his Son" (8:29). As we are conformed more into the likeness of Christ, we are better equipped to see God for who he really is and patiently endure our suffering. The apostle Peter echoed this promise of Christlikeness in his second letter.

> As we know Jesus better, his divine power gives us everything we need for living a godly life…And by that same mighty power, he has given us all of his rich and wonderful promises. He has promised that you will escape the decadence all around you caused by evil desires and that you will share in his divine nature [Christlikeness].

> So make every effort to apply the benefits of those promises to your life. Then your faith will produce a life of moral excellence. A life of moral excellence leads to knowing God better. Knowing God leads to self-control. Self-control leads to patient endurance, and patient endurance leads to godliness. Godliness leads to love for other Christians and finally you will grow to have genuine love for everyone. (2 Peter 1:3–9 NLT*)

To some degree, the above message from God's Word may feel overwhelming. Yet it actually expresses the simplicity of the gospel message, which is this: As God's child, you are in the process of becoming more and more like Jesus through the power of the Holy Spirit. So you don't need to work at becoming more like him in your own strength. In fact, as the above passages show, he takes all the pressure off you by personally teaching you his characteristics, including how to patiently endure suffering.

ASSIGNMENT

Can You Hear Him Calling You?

As you read the following aloud, picture this: Jesus is standing a few feet from you. You're curious, because the Savior is holding a wooden yoke. Jesus' eyes are welcoming, and his smile is warm. You can sense his delight in being there just with you.

From ancient times up through the early twentieth century, a yoke was used to link a pair of horses or oxen so they could pull a farming plow in unison. It was generally made of two wooden U-shaped pieces fastened side by side to a heavy crossbar. A farmer would place a more experienced animal on one side of the yoke and the less experienced on the other. Yoking the two animals together allowed the experienced animal to gently teach and train the younger. By joining the two animals together, the heavy burden was lightened, and the load was shared.

ENCOUNTER JESUS

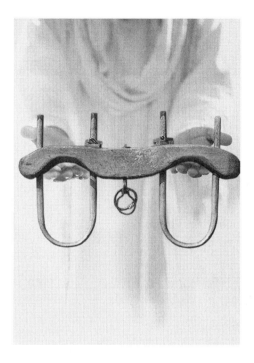

Now imagine Jesus looking tenderly at you as he lifts the yoke toward you as if offering it to you. He gently nods his head and smiles as he says:

> "Come to me, all of you who are weary and carry heavy burdens, and I will give you rest. Take my yoke upon you. Let me teach you, because I am humble and gentle at heart, and you will find rest for your souls. For my yoke is easy to bear, and the burden I give you is light." (Matthew 11:28–30)

Jesus then slips his head into one side of the yoke, points to the empty side, and invites you to be joined together with him. He continues to speak to you.

I know you have been suffering terribly. You have been bearing a heavy burden, and I want to bear it with you.

Now that you are here beside me, we will both bear this burden together. I will teach you to bear it and ease it for you by imparting my life to yours. As we walk through these dark days together, you can hold on to me and experience my strength and support, my patience and comfort, my undying love and unconditional acceptance. I am all that and more to you.

Rely on me. Trust in me. Let go of your own strength and efforts to make it through this hard time and rest in me. As you take hold of me, you will sense my empowering Spirit living in you, transforming you more and more into my likeness.

Will you be yoked with me?

How do you respond to this invitation from Jesus? Put your response in writing.

After your response, let the Holy Spirit encourage your heart with this promise:

Give me happiness, O Lord, for I give myself to you. Oh Lord, you are so good, so ready to forgive, so full of unfailing love for all who ask for your help. (Psalm 86:4–5)

 L3. A Spirit-empowered disciple experiences God as he really is through deepened intimacy with him.

6

Facing the "Guilt" and Regrets of Our Loss

It was Saturday. All of our family was together in the motorhome parked at a retreat center in Georgia. Austin had been out of the hospital for eight months after his second heart transplant. He had his ups and downs, but he seemed improved. Austin and Brianna were back to their lighthearted teasing, and that brought welcome laughter to our lives.

Later that day, Austin began to experience chills and a low-grade fever. I (Cindy) gave him some natural remedies to reduce his symptoms and urged him to stay in bed. During the day, I was baking his favorite sugar/gluten-free peanut butter pie. I hoped he would feel well enough to enjoy it the next day.

When evening came, I felt tired and decided to sleep in the back bedroom while Duane camped out beside Austin's bunk. For the first few hours, Duane got little sleep because Austin kept getting up and down. It was after midnight when he finally settled down, and they both fell asleep.

"Cindy, wake up!" Duane called out as he shook my shoulder. The urgency in his voice startled me.

"He's not breathing. Austin's not breathing."

I immediately jumped out of bed. Duane had made his way back to Austin and had him on the floor frantically performing CPR. I called 911. It was around 2:00 a.m.

The EMS team arrived soon and took over. The ambulance took Austin to a nearby hospital, but it was too late. Our son never regained consciousness. Austin was gone.

The Guilt of "If Only"

The "if-onlys" began almost instantly. *If only* I had alternated with Duane so that one of us would have been awake at all times, perhaps we could have revived Austin. *If only* I had stayed awake rather than selfishly sleeping, I could have been with my son in his last moments of life. I thought, *How could I be baking a pie while my son was obviously breathing his last breaths right in front of me? If only* I had been more attentive and taken him to the doctor when he first got a fever. *If only* I had taken better care of him. If only! If only! If only!

A virus called CMV (cytomegalovirus) had been detected in Austin's blood after his latest heart transplant, and he was taking medication to counteract it. But unknown to anyone, the virus began silently attacking other organs in his body. He died from this CMV infection. There was little that medical professionals could have done to save his life at the point when he began showing symptoms. But that didn't keep me from feeling any less guilty. The if-onlys kept plaguing me.

I threw the peanut butter pie away. It was a long, long time before I could even think of eating that kind of pie again. Nor could I sleep soundly after Austin died. We had two additional small children by then, and I was so afraid to fall into a deep sleep. What if they needed me? My emotional guilt said, "I'm not going to fail them like I failed my son!"

Guilt and self-condemnation tend to worm their way into our psyches and complicate the grieving process. We feel responsible for the losses we have experienced. We may have made certain decisions that we feel somehow contributed indirectly to our loss. These feelings often produce a deep sense of guilt. Rarely does this guilt have merit, yet we irrationally assume blame and bear a load of what is actually false guilt. We tend to beat ourselves up over imagined if-only scenarios and suffer from a heavy overdose of self-condemnation.

"Oh, how I wish I had done things differently. If only this would have happened. If only I had done X, Y, or Z correctly."

The list of if-onlys can be virtually endless:

If only I had...

> *been there more for my loved one.*
>
> *taken better care of myself.*
>
> *been on top of the situation more.*
>
> *been more attentive to the symptoms.*
>
> *contacted the doctor sooner.*
>
> *warned my loved one of certain dangers.*
>
> *not gotten so irritated at times.*
>
> *shown more love and patience.*

The if-onlys are most often expressions of our assumed guilt, which is usually false guilt that piles up around our if-onlys and keeps us from moving forward. Guilt is an impediment to the grief process because it can prevent us from resolving our grief. The first step in letting go of these feelings of guilt is to face them. Once we muster the courage to face them directly, we'll find that most of them aren't even valid. Yet we can't know that until we identify each if-only expression of guilt to determine whether it is valid or false.

ASSIGNMENT

If Only and Not Enough

Complete the following exercise and then discuss it with your journey partner. Take a moment and list some of the if-onlys you have felt surrounding your loss. Granted, this is not an easy exercise, but it is important to bring your if-onlys to the surface. They reveal any sense of responsibility you may feel and any regrets you may have for decisions you made at the time. You can come back to this exercise later and identify more as they come to you. Be honest with yourself as you write out some of your if-onlys.

If only I had...

Now take the step of trying to separate out what is actually true from what is a purely emotional reaction. Just because we feel guilty about our if-onlys doesn't mean we are actually guilty. The feelings of guilt are real feelings, and we may see them as our current reality. But those feelings may not be based on what is actually true.

I felt guilty for not being right there when Austin died. I felt that I had been selfish in trying to get some sleep. I felt guilty for not giving more of my time and energy to him. But was it actually true that I was guilty? No. My feelings of guilt were real, but my reasons for feeling guilt were not. My guilt feelings were not based on truth. It was okay for me to get some rest, and in doing so, I was not guilty of being an irresponsible mother and caregiver to my dying son.

Under the circumstances, you may have done your best to be there, to take care of, and to attend to the needs of your loved one. That may be the actual truth. Yet you may still feel pangs of guilt. Go with what is actually true while still admitting that your feelings of guilt are real. Acknowledge that those feelings are not based on reality, and therefore, you actually carry no blame.

It's natural to want to assign blame. A strong sense of injustice rises to the surface during times of loss. Consciously or subconsciously we may feel that someone or something must be responsible, and we look for a fall guy, even if it ends up being ourselves. Of course, in some cases someone or something may clearly be at fault. But even in those cases where the blame is justly assigned to other people or other causes, we may still transfer part of the blame to ourselves.

Now, take another look at your list of if-onlys, and in each case decide whether or how much you are to take blame. If you're convinced that you are to blame, place a "T" for "True" to the right of the if-only. If you are not to blame, place an "F" for "False." If you are somewhat to blame, place an "M" for "Maybe I am somewhat to blame." This exercise will be useful in the chapter exercises that follow.

The Regrets of "Not Enough"

Having a relationship with someone is an ongoing journey of ups and downs, of healthy growth and occasional setbacks. There are good communications in a relationship. There are also unhealthy communications. There are things said and things left unsaid. When your loved one died, it is unlikely that everything in the relationship was buttoned down and in perfect order. There may have been some things left unsaid that should have been addressed. There may have been some things said that should have been corrected. All relational journeys are imperfect ones because none of us is perfect.

So, it's natural that we would have some regrets surrounding life's losses. We could regret that we…

> didn't do enough.
>
> weren't good enough.
>
> didn't give enough.
>
> weren't there enough.
>
> didn't love enough.
>
> weren't enough period!

Face it. If you truly love someone, you don't want that relational journey to end. But now that it has ended, you may feel that parts of it were not quite complete, and you wish you had been given just a little more time. You wanted the journey to last a little longer so you could bring the relationship to a better close. That's the nature of a relational journey with someone. You want to keep making it better. But since that is no longer possible, you may very well feel that it ended before it was complete, and that brings you regrets. We call these "not-enough" regrets because you feel that whatever you did in your relationship with your loved one was not enough. You regret that there was not enough time for a do-over.

A father shared with us that he had lost his grown daughter. They had a good relationship but not a perfect one because there are no perfect relationships. He told us:

She knew I loved her, and I knew she loved me. But I wish things had been better between us. I wish I had been a better father and friend to my daughter.

I wish I had been a more attentive and tender dad who sat and listened more to her. I wish I had visited with her more, but somehow, I seemed too busy.

She went through some tough times, and I wish I had been there more to comfort her, to support her and make her feel more approved of. I didn't hug her enough or tell her I loved her enough or make her feel I was proud of her enough.

I feel as though I am in an ocean of grief. And these regrets are beginning to haunt me. I feel them pulling me deeper into that bottomless sea.

This father felt the load of his unfinished relational journey with his daughter. And it would have kept him stuck with unresolved grief if he hadn't begun the process of letting go of his regrets. He began to free himself from his regrets by taking the proven steps away from guilt that we will outline for you in this section.

The first step is to identify those regrets as specifically as you can. It isn't an easy process because it is so painful. It is painful to remind ourselves of what we feel we should or should not have done. But unless we identify our regrets, we can't face them and gain freedom from them. That's why identifying them is the starting point.

Now identify some of your regrets by thinking of things that you wish you had said or not said, did or didn't do enough of, should have done more of or done better, and so on. Write your not-enough regrets here.

Here's the good news! If you have identified some of the guilt feelings caused by your if-onlys and the regrets caused by your not-enoughs, you have established the foundation for letting go and being free of them. The next two chapters and the Experiential exercises will open the path to your emotional freedom. It did for us.

Let us pray for you:

> *Lord, you are the God of joy and freedom. Please be with our friends as they continue their journey, specifically to be free of guilt, self-condemnation, and regrets. They have suffered great pain over the loss they have endured. Their relational journey was no doubt incomplete, and they feel a measure of guilt and regret because of it. Please give them strength and courage to move forward and face some unpleasant memories in order to find peace and freedom. Thank you for your tender love and care for our friends. Give them a sense of peace and resolve to continue this grief journey. In your loving name we pray. Amen.*

Close this chapter by meditating on another one of Jesus' prayers for you.

ENCOUNTER JESUS

There is now no condemnation for those who are in Christ Jesus.
ROMANS 8:1 NIV

In Romans 8:33–34, the apostle Paul uses the words *accuse* and *condemn*. These are legal terms you might hear inside a courtroom. So, to receive the full impact of this encounter, we urge you to meditate on this passage as you form a mental picture of a courtroom.

Imagine sitting in the seat of the accused in this courtroom. You feel intimidated by your surroundings. You look around and see the stern faces of people whose words are critical and judgmental. The only voices you hear are ones that accuse and condemn you. You feel yourself sinking deeper and deeper into despair.

Suddenly, Jesus enters the courtroom. You see his flowing robes, sandaled feet, and bearded face. Rather than taking his place behind the judge's bench, Jesus walks toward you, stands by your side, eases his arm around your shoulder, and gently leads you to join him as he kneels in prayer.

You listen carefully and discover that Jesus is praying for you. He's interceding for the needs in your life. He's asking the Father to bring you strength, truth, relief, freedom, and peace. Then you hear him ask, "Where are your accusers?" You glance up and suddenly realize that the courtroom is completely empty. Everyone who was hurling condemnation at you has disappeared from the room. Each voice that brought a charge against you has vanished. Every message of accusation and judgment has been silenced. Jesus then proclaims, "Neither do I accuse you."

Let the truth of this scene impact your heart. The only One who can condemn you is praying for you! The only One who is equipped to bring judgment does not. As you continue working to let go of regret and guilt, don't forget—the Holy One of the universe does not accuse you.

Take the next few moments to express your gratitude and love to Jesus.

Jesus, I am thankful you don't judge or condemn me. In fact, you are praying for me. These truths make me incredibly grateful because…

 W1.   A Spirit-empowered disciple is frequently led by the Spirit into deeper love for the One who wrote the Word.

After you have completed this encounter with Jesus, you may want to invite your journey partner to experience it as well. Share about your personal moments with Jesus. Reaffirm the truth that he has silenced the accusations, if-onlys and regrets. Celebrate together over the One who prays for you!

7

The Power to Live in the Present

"Cindy...Cindy...Are you okay?"

I stirred from my sleep as I felt Duane shaking me. It was yet another one of those dreams that had been plaguing me.

Night after night I had nightmares in which I was never able to keep Austin safe enough to remain with us. It seemed I could never let myself off the hook for not protecting my son from the inevitable.

I was allowing previous events and painful memories to hold me hostage to the past, which prevented me from living my life in the present. It was as if my emotions were demanding that time turn backward to undo what had already happened. Deep inside I was crying out to change the unchangeable. It made no rational sense, of course, and it was clearly impossible. Yet I was stuck because I wanted what I would never have—to change the past in order to get a different outcome in my present.

We Only Have This Moment

There is an obvious fact that makes so much sense, yet we rarely seem to think about it. It's this: The only moment we have to live is the one we're living now in the present.

Whenever I am regretting the past and dredging up painful memories, I am failing to live in the present. In those moments, my emotions are being pulled back into the past to relive those painful events. This does not mean that we can or should shut the past out of our minds. We have a memory, and memories cannot be eradicated. To get unstuck from the painful past, I must go through the process of feeling it fully in order to continually experience comfort and healing. But like any process, we have to *go through it* before we can emerge into healing. It really helped me to realize that the process of letting go and holding on was a process that would allow me to live more fully in the present.

Songwriter Gloria Gaither captured this truth in the lyrics of her song "We Have This Moment, Today": "Yesterday's gone, and tomorrow may never come, but we have this moment today." Yesterday is our past. Tomorrow is our future. It is only in today—our present—that we can truly live a life of joy and peace.

Dr. David Augsburger, author of the timeless book *Caring Enough to Forgive*, writes: "If I am willing to let go of the past without trying to change the unchangeable, and accept the future without hoping to control the uncontrollable, I will be able to live now, which is the only time for living that I have."[6] Holding on to my past pain and fretting about the future without Austin was exhausting—it kept me from living in the now.

A. A. Milne wrote a children's book back in 1926 entitled *Winnie-the-Pooh*. Today Pooh is a classic character who has been credited with many profound quotes, two of which come from the movie *Christopher Robin*. These quotes are particularly insightful in the way they address our attempt to be free to live our lives in the present. Pooh pointed out: "Yesterday, when it was tomorrow, was too much day for me. But today, that's my favorite day." He went on to say, "Yesterday is history, tomorrow is a mystery, but today is a gift. That's why we call it the present."[7]

The present is a gift—a gift from God. And Pooh is right: yesterday, when it was tomorrow, is too much day for us. Memories of yesterday and anticipation of tomorrow are by no means wrong. But they can become too much for us when they are so filled with fear and pain that they keep us from experiencing the joy of our present.

In my continued grieving and as I received comfort from God and other people, I began to let go of a past existence that I knew I could no longer experience with Austin. It was then that I began to take hold of a life that I could live in the present without my son. I was slowly learning how to honor his memory that was in my past while honoring the truth that he was no longer in my present. My heart was beginning to experience healing. But I do not believe that process could have begun without a critical step that involved claiming a certain promise in my present. It was the promise of forgiveness—especially of forgiving myself.

The Power of Forgiveness

How could I let go of my sense of guilt brought on by my if-onlys? How could I let go of the regrets of my not-enoughs? The reality was, as a perfectionist, I chided myself for not being the perfect mother to my son. It's true that I got tired and asked for an occasional reprieve from constantly caring for Austin. At times I did lose patience. I wasn't always the sweetest caregiver. My list of faults and failures could go on. The point is, I had regrets and feelings of guilt—true guilt and false guilt. We all have them.

To let go of our regrets and guilt solely by our human strength is impossible. We need the power that comes from taking hold of forgiveness. It is the actual experience of being forgiven that empowers us to let go of our regrets and feelings of guilt. The very essence of being forgiven is to be released of blame and set free of guilt. Being set free of your guilt and regrets enables you to be set free of past pain so you can live in the moment and enjoy the gift of the present. That is what's needed to help you move forward to a new normal.

Yet one problem with this may seem obvious to you. The one you lost isn't here to forgive you. So how can forgiveness even be possible?

The amazing truth is that we do not need the response of the person we are seeking forgiveness from in order to be forgiven. In fact, even if a living person refuses our request for forgiveness, that doesn't keep us from receiving forgiveness. This is true because God is the ultimate source of our forgiveness. This means we can be released from the guilt of our offense toward another regardless of the human response. We can find release and freedom from guilt by claiming the promise of Scripture that says, "If we confess our sins to him [our guilty feelings and regrets], he is faithful and just to forgive us our sins" (1 John 1:9). Since God promises to be faithful and just to forgive us, the human relationship with our lost loved one can be mended and made complete from our perspective despite the fact that he or she cannot respond.

Take a moment to go back to the previous chapter and look over your "If-Only and Not-Enough" lists. In some of those cases, you may be struggling with real guilt; in other cases, it may be false guilt. In either case, you need to find release and freedom from your guilt and regrets. Now, in the spaces that follow, take each of your if-onlys and not-enoughs from the previous chapter and rephrase them in the form of a confession. Here are some examples from my own life.

God, as I reflect on my loss and my responsibilities:

- Please forgive me for not being at Austin's side when he breathed his last breath.

- Forgive me for baking him a pie when I should have been attending to his needs.

- Forgive me for not being attentive enough to recognize how critically sick he was.

- Forgive me for the times I became impatient with him.

- Forgive me for being too busy to have more quality fun times with him.

ASSIGNMENT

Taking Hold of Forgiveness

Complete the following assignment and then share it with your journey partner. Take time to list your own "Please forgive me" statements taken from what you wrote in Chapter 6. Write them out here, make them your prayer, and thank God for forgiving you.

The important truth of your confessions is that God knows you, hears you, and promises to forgive you. *Let go* **of your guilt and regrets.** *Take hold* **of God's forgiveness and allow his grace and mercy to flood your soul even to the extent of forgiving yourself.**

Taking Hold of Forgiveness and Forgiving Yourself

Regardless of your offenses, God doesn't hold back or become reluctant to forgive you. Therefore, you should never hesitate to accept his forgiveness. He freely offers it, so freely receive it. But sometimes the hesitancy to receive his forgiveness is from within—we fail to forgive ourselves.

Forgiving ourselves of our past regrets and shortcomings requires another act of letting go. This might be difficult because those things we said and did or didn't say or do may seem deeply intertwined. We feel that we are letting go of who we were with the one we lost. In that sense, forgiving ourselves can make us feel that we're apologizing for the connection we had with our loved one. Who wants to do that? So, we need to separate our past performance—which needs forgiveness—from our personhood. Making this distinction between "what we've done" and "who we are" is precisely what God does. He sees our actions separate from the essence of who we are and removes "our sins as far away from us as the east is from the west" (Psalm 103:12 TLB).

Our true intentions were probably never to hurt our loved one in the first place. God sees our repentant heart and forgives every regretted act that has burdened us with feelings of guilt. Scripture says, "God made you alive with Christ, for he forgave all our sins. He canceled the record of the charges against us and took it away by nailing it to the cross" (Colossians 2:13–14).

Who are we to disagree with God? That's what we do when we won't forgive ourselves. He says we are forgiven. That's a truth to hold on to.

One of the best ways to forgive ourselves is to express gratitude to Jesus for dying for us and taking away our sins. A heart that is grateful to our merciful God can melt our self-condemnation away and allow his forgiveness to go so deep that it eradicates all condemnation—including self-condemnation. This makes forgiving ourselves a natural consequence of God's forgiveness. We simply follow his lead.

As far as God is concerned, all of your offenses, large and small, have been canceled out, and God no longer even remembers them. "I will forgive their wickedness," God says, "and I will never again remember their sins" (Jeremiah 31:34). "I—yes, I alone—will blot out your sins for my sake and will never think of them again" (Isaiah 43:25). "But God showed his great love for us by sending Christ to die for us while we were still sinners" (Romans 5:8).

Every act of impatience, unkind word, lack of affection, if only, and not enough is now gone and not even remembered by God. It has been dissolved in his sea of forgiveness and forgetfulness. Through the grace of God's forgiveness and the empowerment of his Spirit, you are free to let go of all feelings of guilt and regret. As you loosen your hold on your past hurts, you can reach out and take hold of your forgiveness and begin to truly live in the present. Remember, letting go of your guilt and regrets is not a one-time act. It is an ongoing process of repeatedly holding on to God's forgiveness and celebrating that you are choosing to forgive yourself.

Let's make this personal. Pause and spend a moment holding on to God's forgiveness.

EXPERIENCE SCRIPTURE

God made him who had no sin to be sin for us,
so that in him we might become the righteousness of God.
2 Corinthians 5:21 NIV

Pause and remember the words Jesus cried out to his Father from the cross: "My God, my God, why have you forsaken me?" (Matthew 27:46 NIV). As Jesus took our sin on himself, the Father, in his holiness, had to turn away from his Son. The One who had no sin became sin for us. The good news of the gospel is that miraculously, through the power of the Holy Spirit, Christ was resurrected and lives again!

Reflect once more on the reason *why* Christ became sin. To make it even more personal, reflect on the question: For whom did he do it? Who benefits from his death and his resurrection?

Quietly listen to God's Spirit whisper the answer to your soul: *He did it for you. He did it for you!* The One who knew no sin became sin for you. If Jesus did not need to die for any other person in the whole world, he would have died for you—and he did die for you. You are one of his beloved. He was raised for you. And because of Christ's gift, you now have the power of the resurrection living in you.

As you meditate on these truths, you might find it helpful to whisper the words, "He did it just for me."

Share your gratitude with God.

Lord, I am so grateful that...

I choose to hold on to the truth of your forgiveness. I choose to hold on to the gift of your Son and marvel that you did it for me!

Finally, take a moment to thank God for your journey so far. Tell him you are claiming his promises. Praise him with the words of the psalmist David: "Oh, what joy for those whose disobedience is forgiven, whose sin [of regrets are] put out of sight! Yes, what joy for those whose record the Lord has cleared of guilt" (Psalm 32:1–2). Jesus reminds us: "I have told you this so that my joy may be in you and that your joy may be complete [in the present]" (John 15:11 NIV).

 W6. A Spirit-empowered disciple encounters Jesus in the Word for deepened transformation in Christ-likeness.

8

Facing the Good and Not So Good about Our Loved One

"Dad, I'm scared."

Austin and I were on the back porch as he began to open up about his fears. A few months earlier, we had learned his heart was failing again. At thirteen years old, he comprehended the prognosis and understood how truly dire it was.

At that moment, Cindy stepped out onto the porch. Seeing the sober expressions on our faces, she asked, "What's going on?"

Instantly Austin burst into tears. I wrapped my arm around my son and pulled him close. Cindy sat down on the other side of him and took his hand in hers. "What is it, Austin? Tell me what's wrong," she urged, gently.

Austin wiped his eyes with his free hand. "Dad and I started talking about my heart and about this latest diagnosis," he said sniffing through his tears, "and what it all might mean."

He was silent for a moment, then he continued, "I really could die, couldn't I?" He looked at Cindy with glistening, red-rimmed eyes. "Mom, I know that if I die, I will go to heaven; that doesn't scare me. But there's so much I still want to do with you and Dad and my sisters. I want to be well and carry my load in this family. I just get so tired of being sick! I…" His voice broke suddenly as he sat silently between us. His shoulders began to heave as he sobbed quietly. We both sat silently with him, holding our son and comforting him with our gentle touch and flowing tears.

Beneath my calm exterior, my mind was racing for an answer, any answer: *Lord, what do I say? I want to help Austin understand, but how can I when I don't fully understand myself?* After a few moments, I spoke.

"Austin," I said softly. He looked up. "I wish I could promise you right here that you won't die, but I can't because I don't know. Neither does your mom. Only God knows. We have to trust in him and try to be content with that. I know that doesn't feel like enough, but sometimes that is all we have."

By this time Austin had gained a little composure. "I'd like to pray," he said. "Lord," he began, "sometimes I really hate being sick so much, and I don't understand what's going on right now. But I know you do. So I am going to trust you. My life is yours, to give or to take, and I know that whatever happens will be for our good and your glory."

When he finished his prayer, Austin looked at us, smiling through his tears. "I'm okay now," he assured us. "I still don't understand what's going on or why, but one thing I do know is that God is right here with me. And that's enough for now."

As a father, I am so proud that I had a son with such courage, faith, a love for God and his family, and such an optimistic view of life. He suffered so much, yet he faced his suffering with an almost eternal sense of strength and hope. Even at the end he seemed so positive and realistic about the bleak prognosis.

Just before being wheeled in for his second transplant at the age of sixteen, Austin said, "I'm not afraid. Just think about it. If I make it through this surgery, I get to spend more time with my family and more time sharing God's love with others. And if I don't make it, I get to be in heaven with my heavenly Father. You see, I'm a winner either way!"

Verbalizing the Good

Most of us failed to say everything we wanted to say to our loved one before the end. One of my own regrets is that I didn't verbalize my feelings to my son as much as I wanted. The process that brings greater closure and deals with our unresolved grief is to verbalize our love for the one we lost.

Think of the positive qualities your loved one had—including character qualities, skills, and special giftedness. We loved the ones we lost not because of how well they performed or what they accomplished but because of who they were at the core of their being. That is what we loved—we loved the person.

We may not have verbalized our appreciation for those qualities as much as we would have liked, but we can do it now. And when we do, it reinforces our heart memories of our loved ones and confirms to our emotions that we will never, ever forget them or fail to be thankful for who they were.

This verbal heart reinforcement can be expressed by completing statements such as "I loved your…"; "I was so proud of…"; and "You brought such joy to me when…"

For example, in my own case I can say:

- Austin, I loved your tender heart and how compassionate you were to others in need.

- Son, I was so proud of the courage you displayed in the face of pain and death.

- Austin, you brought joy to me when you expressed such gratefulness to your mother and sisters when they attended to you. You didn't take them for granted, and that touched me deeply.

I could go on and on. What a blessing it was to spend the almost seventeen years with my son. When I verbalize his exceptional qualities, it assures my emotions that he will always be in my heart.

ASSIGNMENT

Verbalize the Good

Complete the following exercise on your own and then share it with your journey partner. Take a few minutes to reflect on the positive qualities your loved one exhibited. Write several of them. Finish these statements:

I loved your...

I was so proud of...

You brought such joy to me when...

Now, verbalize what you wrote above in a prayer. Read each statement aloud and thank God you had the time with your loved one that you did.

After your time in prayer, look for and seize opportunities to repeat these words of affirmation as you tell others about your loved one. Tell what made your loved one special and so significant to you.

Verbalizing the Humanity of Our Loved One

When was the last time you met an absolutely perfect person? This individual would naturally be the sweetest, kindest, most selfless, caring, and loving person in the world. Of course, you and I have never met such a human because no one like that exists.

Yet we may tend to idealize the loved one we lost. We might place a rosy gloss over the shortcomings of our lost one for a number of reasons, but the most common one is because we feel guilty for our relational failures and lapses—our if-onlys and not-enoughs. The reality is, however, that those shortcomings, failures, miscommunications, and hurtful feelings probably worked both ways. It's highly likely that your lost loved one did not possess the perfection that your selective memory chooses to present to your mind.

It may be difficult to acknowledge that the relational journey with your loved one was imperfect and that part of that imperfection actually belongs to them. They would have their own set of if-onlys and not-enoughs to deal with.

The loved ones we lost weren't perfect. Their imperfections may have varied from a set of minor irritations or frustrations to serious issues causing real problems and deep pain. Whatever the case, we don't have to remain stuck in unresolved grief due to unfinished relational business with our loved one. We can let go and forgive them. The amazing truth is that we don't even need to hear our loved ones say, "Please forgive me for…" in order to forgive them. We have the power to forgive—regardless of whether they ask it or not. We can claim God's promise:

> Make allowance for each other's faults, and forgive anyone who offends you. Remember the Lord forgave you, so you must forgive others. Above all, clothe yourself in love, which binds us all together in perfect harmony. (Colossians 3:13–14)

At first blush, this passage may not appear to be a promise. But it is. God's forgiveness of you and your forgiveness of others are linked. When you accept God's forgiveness, you experience his amazing grace and mercy. As a result, you "must (can do nothing less than) forgive others." Why? That is the empowering nature of grace and mercy. When you have been given loving grace and mercy so freely, you are empowered to freely give loving grace and mercy to others. Your joy at receiving the gift compels you to pass it along. And this is where we find the promise. When we pass to others the grace and mercy God gives us, his love "binds us all together in perfect harmony" (v. 14). That love and forgiveness you extend toward your loved one promise to bring greater completion and a renewed sense of wholeness to your own life.

ASSIGNMENT

Forgive as You've Been Forgiven

Complete the following exercise and then discuss it with your journey partner. Take a moment and think of those areas in which your loved one may have offended you, hurt you, or done something wrong. Those offenses may be major, minor, or somewhere in between.

Just as you have been freely forgiven by God, freely forgive your loved one. Verbalize your forgiveness by reading the following declaration aloud. Pause and verbalize your choice to forgive your loved one. Tell the Lord about this decision.

Lord, I choose to share the forgiveness you have given me with _____. I choose to forgive him/her for...

Depending on our situation, there may be others we need to forgive. The death of our loved one may have been caused in whole or in part by a drunk or reckless driver, improper actions by a medical staff, a mistaken or late diagnosis, ineffective medication, or something similar. We may blame and carry resentment toward someone for the death. Or we may still struggle with blaming God.

If you hold blame or resentment toward others for your loved one's death, you can forgive and release them as well. Even if they truly do bear blame, you can still choose to forgive.

In the space below, list those whom you may blame for their part in your loved one's death. After each name, write, "I forgive you."

As you work on the next exercise, remember once again that you have been freely forgiven; therefore, freely forgive. Verbalize your forgiveness by reading aloud what you wrote above, followed by your choice to forgive.

Through God's empowering grace and mercy, we encourage you to:

> **Let go** **of any resentment, irritation, displeasure, dissatisfaction, or ill feelings you may have had toward your loved one or anyone else, and** **take hold** **of a forgiving spirit—forgive as you have been forgiven.**

Like all facets of our journey to resolve our grief, forgiveness is a process. As things come to mind in the future that require your forgiveness, forgive as you have been forgiven. We must forgive and keep on forgiving.

> God blesses those who are merciful, for they will be shown mercy. (Matthew 5:7)

> O Lord, you are so good, so ready to forgive. (Psalm 86:5)

> [Peter asked,] "Lord, how often should I forgive someone who sins against me? Seven times?" "No, not seven times," Jesus replied, "but seventy times seven!" (Matthew 18:21–22) [Our forgiveness is to be ongoing. Jesus is saying, "Hold on to your forgiving spirit."]

> Love is patient and kind…It does not demand its own way. It is not irritable, and it keeps no record of being wronged [love forgives and keeps on forgiving]. (1 Corinthians 13:4–5)

Let's continue to take hold of forgiveness by spending time with Jesus—our Advocate.

ENCOUNTER JESUS

"I will send you the Advocate—the Spirit of truth.
He will come to you from the Father and will testify all about me."
JOHN 15:26

In the next few minutes, ask the Holy Spirit to be your Advocate for forgiveness and freedom. Ask him to reveal the truest needs of your life that are connected to the circumstances of your grief. What needs and challenges are you facing that depend on the empowerment of his forgiveness, healing, and hope?

Now, ask the Holy Spirit about the character of Jesus. Ask him to reveal more about Jesus to you. Does the Spirit want you to know that Jesus is the All-Powerful One, the Mighty Counselor, or the Comforter? Does he want you to be reminded that he is the God of restoration and the ultimate provider of grace and forgiveness? One of the Spirit's functions is to reveal to you more of Jesus, so ask him in faith to do just that.

> *Holy Spirit—my Advocate—given the needs of my life and the challenges of unforgiveness I face, what do you want to share with me about Jesus? What do you want me to know about him?*

Listen as the Spirit testifies about Jesus, and then be open to what he wants for you. Listen as he might ask you to deepen your forgiveness of others, promise the healing of your heart, comfort your pain, and then renew your hope.

 L2. A Spirit-empowered disciple listens to God for direction and discernment.

ENCOUNTER JESUS FOR THE JOURNEY PARTNER

"As I have loved you, so you must love one another."
JOHN 13:34 NIV

With this one verse, Jesus was both reminding the disciples about all the ways that he had loved them, as well as foreshadowing his upcoming display of love on Calvary. How Christ loves is without comparison. In this same verse, Jesus also gave us a clue as to how his love is supposed to impact our lives and the world in which we live. He wants us to soak up his love deeply and personally and then demonstrate that same love to others. Receive his love and then show it to others.

As you make yourself available to your grieving friend and prepare to listen to their assignments and reflections, spend a few moments remembering how Jesus has loved you. Reflect on just a few aspects of his love:

- God has shown his love to you by *sacrificing his Son* to die for you. While you were still going your own way and separated from God, he sent Jesus to die just for you. His love is without condition, demand, or expectation. He loved you *before* you had straightened out your life. He sacrificed for you *while* you were still in the mess of your sin. He freely gave his love because you are loved by God (Romans 5:8).

- God has shown his love to you by being *present with you* at every moment of every day. Nothing can separate you from his love. Nothing you do can change his love. His love cannot be lost, lessened, or diminished. It is forever yours because you are loved by God (8:38–39).

Reflect on some of the ways God has loved you, and then thank him for some specific aspect of his love that has great meaning for you.

I am especially thankful for the truth that God loves me by _____ because …

Now, let your love for your grieving friend be a reflection of how God loves you. As your friend shares their responses to the exercises in this section, be prepared to love unconditionally, sacrificially, and without demand or expectation. Be present with your friend. Don't let anything distract you or diminish your expression of love. Because you have received God's love, show it to others.

 L4. A Spirit-empowered disciple rejoices regularly in his or her identity as God's beloved.

9

Feeling Uncertain about the Future

She was the picture of health!

Within two years of Austin's birth, God blessed us with our eight pound, nine ounce, beautiful baby daughter, Brianna. Even with the challenges of Austin's heart transplant, he was growing into a happy little boy. And now with the birth of a healthy baby girl I (Cindy) felt encouraged. Life was getting back to normal.

When Brianna was two years old, our third child, Alisha, was born. She weighed only five pounds, eight ounces. The doctors surmised that she hadn't gotten all the nourishment she needed toward the end of the pregnancy. But she began to gain weight in the weeks that followed, so we were hopeful.

Two months later, Duane and I attended the wedding of a friend in North Carolina. I noticed that Alisha seemed lethargic and was coughing a good bit. To be safe, we decided to take her to the ER.

As we headed to the hospital, I was optimistic that our little girl had nothing more than bronchitis. As the emergency doctor examined Alisha, she was alert, looking around, and smiling. To be thorough, the doctor ordered an X-ray of her chest.

As I sat waiting for the results, I cradled Alisha in my arms. She seemed so much better. Duane stood near me, smiling at our little girl.

As the doctor entered the room, he was slowly shaking his head. "I'm sorry to tell you this...," he began as Duane and I held our breath, "but your little girl has a very enlarged heart."

My own heart fell to my stomach. Duane reached for a chair and sat down. Neither of us could believe what we were hearing. Was another one of our children suffering from a severe heart condition? Could all this be happening again? How serious was it?

It was determined that we needed to get Alisha into a hospital with a pediatric ICU. I rode in the back of the ambulance during the transport to a larger hospital, holding Alisha close. *Lord*, I prayed, *don't let this be a serious condition. Please heal my little girl. I can't lose my little girl.*

Upon arriving at the hospital, I was led to the ICU. It wasn't long before Duane joined me in consultation with the cardiologist. As the doctor viewed the X-rays, I heard him mutter under his breath, "I've never seen anything like this."

He turned to us, "I'm sorry, but your child's heart is extremely enlarged. Her heart is the size of *your* fist, Mrs. Mullett, when it should be the size of her own fist. There's nothing we can do short of a heart transplant."

As the day wore on, Alisha worsened. She was kept overnight in the hospital, and the next morning she crashed. Once again one of our children had to be put on life support to be kept alive. One of the attending cardiologists had also seen Austin and knew our story. She approached Duane and me, her hands trembling, "I want to be upfront with you. It doesn't look like your little girl is going to make it."

"What about a heart transplant?" Duane asked.

"It's possible but not probable," the doctor replied.

Even though Alisha was put on the heart transplant list, we were given little hope. Despite all the doctors could do, her little body was steadily declining. We knew Alisha didn't have long. The emotional pain was almost unbearable. We waited. We prayed. We hoped somehow God would intervene on behalf of our little girl. Our prayer was, *God, if someone chooses to be generous in their time of loss, we'll thank you for that, but if not, we will thank you for the three months you've given Alisha to us.* Three weeks later we got the word: "We have a donor heart for your daughter."

The night before Alisha's transplant, she lay in her bed with a heart rate well over two hundred. We could hear her grunting and see her little body fluttering and shaking with every breath. I didn't know how she could survive even one more day.

The transplant surgery was successful, and eventually we were able to bring Alisha home from the hospital. Without consciously realizing it at the time, we were suffering a loss—the loss of a healthy family. We tried to move forward as normally as possible, but down deep, fear was gripping my heart. As a mother, I was constantly vigilant and protective of the physical environment of my children. With two having suppressed immune systems, I was on guard every minute, afraid for them to be around anyone who even sneezed or coughed. The future of our family felt uncertain. I couldn't imagine how things could get any worse. But they did.

When Alisha was two and a half, she complained to me about an itch. I noticed a rash on her arm that I thought needed medical attention.

We took Alisha to an allergy doctor who found that she was allergic to almost everything. It quickly became a challenge to know what to feed her because of her severe food allergies. The test also revealed she had multiple chemical sensitivities and was reacting to many things in the environment. As the weeks and months went by, she got progressively worse. By the time Alisha was three years old, she had scalp buildup so severe that she would wake up in the morning with her hair in mats. I tried several different treatments, but not one was effective. It eventually reached the point where I had to cut Alisha's hair as close to the scalp as possible so that air could get to it and relieve some of her pain.

Alisha's condition worsened to the point that her skin itched all the time. She scratched constantly, often until she bled. It got so bad that she screamed in pain every time she got a bath because the water burned her skin. By the time Alisha was four years old, her skin had gotten so tender that she was unable to walk. There were deep cracks in the bend of her knees. My precious little girl was almost unrecognizable. Her eyes were swollen shut, her mouth was only able to open up enough to sip from a straw, and her skin was broken and oozing. When Alisha caught a glimpse of herself in a mirror, she was so horrified that she had to fight rising nausea.

Doctors eventually recommended the use of a hyperbaric oxygen chamber. Larger hospitals use these for burn and deep-wound patients. High pressure pushes oxygen deep into the plasma, which promotes healing. Over time, the treatments in the hyperbaric oxygen chamber, various nutritional therapies, and a new house built with allergy-free materials enabled Alisha to eventually recover. But just as she was recovering, Austin was diagnosed with his first round of cancer. The whole ordeal of ups and downs left me feeling uncertain and fearful of the future.

Loss and Fear of Tomorrow

After a major loss, it's natural to feel anxiety and to fear what's going to happen next. It's common to sense that certain goals, dreams, and plans have vanished. We can feel that we have lost control of our life, and that can cause fear.

Another fallout of the 2020 COVID-19 pandemic was the global sense of fear and uncertainty. Lives were turned upside down as many confirmed cases were reported worldwide. Entire countries locked down. World stock markets plunged, thousands of small businesses failed or were on the brink, unemployment rose to heights our country had not seen since the Great Depression of the 1930s, and people had no sense of what to expect next. Some have referred to the COVID-19 pandemic as the Great Disruption.

Life becomes uncertain when our present day is disrupted and our future is unknown. The painful losses of yesterday can even intensify our uncertainty. In the midst of grief, struggle, or disruption, the uneasiness we feel today is often compounded because it threatens to show up tomorrow. The result? Our security becomes shaken. When fear persists, we feel anxious, and it shatters our emotional peace of mind.

Anxiety and fear may cause these kinds of questions to haunt us: "What will I do now? What will happen to me? How can I go on without the loved one I lost? Will I lose someone or something else? What if I can't move forward? Will I live in a constant state of fear and anxiety? What if my friends abandon me?"

A continual sense of fear and anxiety can paralyze us. It may lead us to doubt and squelch any sense of hope for tomorrow. We can become overwhelmed with a sense of insecurity. And that can rob us of the joy of living in the present.

Security and Peace of Mind

Yes, we may have lost predictability in our life, and our fear and anxiety may fuel a deep sense of insecurity. That is understandable. What we need is an emotional anchor—a strong sense of security that restores to our emotions the certainty that we have cause to feel safe. Our spirit needs to be reinforced with the assurance that we will be provided for, cared for, and protected in the future. That is what brings emotional peace of mind.

We can experience that kind of security and peace of mind by claiming and holding on to some very specific promises in our present. We realize that when you are in the depths of pain and uncertainty, this admonition can seem trite and glib. We know that healing is neither instantaneous nor simple. The issue of fear is real and deserves more serious attention than a simple admonition to "trust God and all will be well." Yet we know from personal experience that an active faith in our very personal and sovereign God can and will bring you a solid sense of security and emotional peace of mind.

When Jesus was on earth, he had a group of followers who were rightly convinced that he was their Messiah. As such, they expected him to overthrow the Romans and establish the Jewish kingdom right then and there. But Jesus told these loyal followers that it was not yet time for him to set up his earthly kingdom. Instead, he would be crucified, rise again, go to his Father, and return someday in the future to set up his kingdom. That meant his followers would have to deal with the continued oppression of the Romans and persecution from the Jewish leaders. As you would expect, this news made them feel insecure and fearful. To dispel those fears, Jesus told them: "I am leaving you with a gift—peace of mind and heart. And the peace I give is a gift the world cannot give. So don't be troubled or afraid" (John 14:27).

Jesus went on to elaborate, telling them that having this peace of mind and heart didn't mean they would be free of pain or suffering. He said: "I am not alone because the

Father is with me. I have told you all this so that you may have peace in me. Here on this earth you will have many trials and sorrow. But take heart, because I have overcome the world" (16:32–33).

We have reason to "take heart." Our peace of mind is rooted in One who has overcome death and has prepared a bright future for us. That future may not arrive as soon as we would like, but eventually it will come, and we will be blessed. That's a promise we can claim and hold on to.

God also made a promise to the children of Israel that we can claim as our own. It is a promise that casts out fear of the unknown. It happened to be Austin's favorite Scripture passage.

> "For I know the plans I have for you," says the Lord. "They are plans
> for good and not for disaster, to give you a future and a hope. In those
> days when you pray, I will listen. If you look for me wholeheartedly,
> you will find me. I will be found by you," says the Lord. "I will end your
> captivity and restore your fortunes." (Jeremiah 29:11–14)

Your fears may hold you captive for a time. And the loss of your loved one may have shattered your relational fortunes. But God has plans for you. They involve a new future and a renewed hope of a life without fear and anxiety.

Your fears can be cast out as you hear God's words and hold on to the truth that he loves you and has already secured your future in him.

Listen to the heart of King David when he expressed the solution to his anxieties and fears:

> When I worried about many things, your assuring words soothed
> my soul. (Psalm 94:19 GW)

> I prayed to the Lord, and he answered me. He freed me from all my
> fears. (34:4)

Our souls are soothed by the assurances that God's Word gives us. When we believe God hears us, we can become free of our fears. That is not just a platitude. That is not mere spiritualizing. That is practical. It works in real life where the rubber meets the road. We can experience peace of mind in the midst of our loss. We encourage you to:

> **Let go of anxieties and fears of the future, and *hold on* to the assurance that God is with you and loves you no matter what.**

No doubt, more fears and anxieties will plague you in the days ahead. Each day, hold on to the assurance for *that* day that God is there for you no matter what. Grasp that promise tightly and keep holding on to the promise that his perfect love can overcome your fear (1 John 4:18–19).

Hold on to His Peace

There is yet another practical step we can take in letting go of our fears and anxieties about tomorrow. Jesus wants us to experience peace of mind in him (John 14:27). He says, "take heart," "don't be troubled or afraid," and "have peace in me." The apostles were able to capture that truth, claim his promises, and experience that peace. Throughout the New Testament they link peace of mind with holding on to a very important condition of the heart. Here are just two examples from Scripture.

> Don't worry about anything; instead, pray about everything. Tell God what you need, and thank him for all he has done. Then you will experience God's peace, which exceeds anything we can understand. His peace will guard your hearts and minds as you live in Christ Jesus. (Philippians 4:6–7)

> Let the peace that comes from Christ rule in your hearts. For as members of one body you are called to live in peace. And always be thankful. (Colossians 3:15)

Did you notice how these two passages advocate a heart exercise that results in a heart condition? The exercise is holding on to a grateful heart and being thankful. The result is peace of mind. The exercise and the condition are linked, especially as we embrace Paul's admonition to pray about everything (Philippians 4:6).

It may seem strange to suggest we cultivate and hold on to a grateful heart in the midst of the agony of our loss. But the apostles understood that peace is empowered by a grateful heart, especially when we're going through dark times. King David acknowledged receiving this empowerment when he said, "I will be glad and rejoice in your unfailing love, for you have seen my troubles, and you care about the anguish of my soul" (Psalm 31:7).

Social scientists claim there are at least twenty-nine scientifically proven benefits for those who express a heart of gratitude. Dr. Robert Emmons, a leading scientific expert on gratitude, asserts that hundreds of studies have shown the emotional, social, psychological, and physical benefits of being grateful. Here are a few of those benefits:

- Makes us happier

- Reduces symptoms of depression

- Increases our resilience to bounce back and recover quickly from setbacks

- Improves sleep

- Reduces pain

- Lowers blood pressure

- Lowers stress

- Makes us more humble, understanding, and compassionate

- Makes us more giving and less self-centered

- Improves relationships[8]

This isn't about denying our grief, burying our feelings of loss, and putting on a happy face. It's about cultivating a grateful heart to God in spite of what we face in life. "Be thankful in all circumstances," Scripture tells us, "for this is God's will for you who belong to Christ Jesus" (1 Thessalonians 5:18).

Take an intentional step toward holding on to trust that God has your present and future in his hands by spending time reflecting on his Word.

EXPERIENCE SCRIPTURE

Whatever was written in earlier times was written for our instruction,
so that through perseverance and the encouragement of the Scriptures
we might have hope.
ROMANS 15:4 NASB

Scripture is an encouragement to our soul. God's words inspire hope and trust in his promises. Here are some of the ways that God wants to encourage your hope and trust. As you persevere in your journey, hold on to the hope of his Word.

- You might say, "This is impossible."
  God says, "Nothing is impossible with me" (Luke 18:27).

- When you say, "I'm too weary. I give up."
  God says, "I will give you rest" (Matthew 11:28–30).

- If you say, "I can't go on."
  God says, "My grace is enough. You can do it" (2 Corinthians 12:9).

- You might say, "I can't make it. There's no way."
  God says, "I've got what you need" (Isaiah 40:28–29).

- When you say, "I'm not able."
  God says, "I AM able. I've got this" (2 Corinthians 9:8).

- If you say, "No one gets it. No one understands."
  God says, "I have heard you, and I will be with you" (Psalm 10:17; 91:15).

After reflecting on the promises above and the hope we can have in God's Word, declare your gratitude and your trust.

God, thank you for being a God who...

I'm especially grateful for this word of encouragement because...

Because of your promise to _____I want to trust you more in...

Give thanks for everything to God the Father in the name of our Lord Jesus Christ. (Ephesians 5:20)

 M6. A Spirit-empowered disciple bears witness of a confident peace and expectant hope in God's lordship in all things.

10

In Good Hands

It had been an anxiety-filled day. I (Cindy) had spent the entire day in the hospital with Austin. He was there to begin anti-rejection treatments because his body was beginning to reject his new heart.

The plan was for Duane to remain at the hospital with him for the next few days. I would go home for some rest and time with our girls. It was a two-and-a-half-hour drive home, so I had some extra time to think and pray.

I thought about where we were in life. I loved my husband and my children, but the thirteen years we had spent as a family were filled with uncertainty. We experienced almost constant stress and many chaotic moments when we had to drop everything immediately and rush one of our children to the hospital. Our life seemed out of control.

When you've lost control of your life, you tend to get fearful. And at this point I felt out of control and full of fear of the future. I was coming to the end of myself.

The raw emotions of it all began to overwhelm me, and I began to weep. Brushing away my tears with one hand even as I tried to concentrate on my driving, I prayed, *Lord, I can't handle this alone. I know you are here with me. Let me feel your presence. Let Austin feel your presence.*

While passing a bank, a large sculpture caught my eye. It was of a huge hand, cupped but holding nothing. I suddenly saw in my mind's eye God's hand with Austin nestled in it. At that moment I felt the Lord say to me, *I love Austin more than you do. He is my son also, and he is in my hand. Trust me to take care of him.*

Perhaps I shouldn't have been surprised by that truth, but it shocked me. I guess it hadn't really dawned on me how deeply and personally God felt about my son. Sure, I knew that God cared about us, even though I couldn't really understand why we had to go through all this suffering. But the thought of God telling me that Austin was his son too hit me hard. If the sovereign God of the universe sees my son as his son too and if he loves him even more than I do, then that changes everything. That means Austin is in the best hands possible.

As I wept, I felt my heart release Austin—I let my son go into God's hands. I spoke out loud and said, *God, Austin does belong to you. You're right.* You *are his Father, and he is* your *son. So I give my dear Austin to* you.

With those surrendering words, I let go and entrusted my son into the hands of God.

Overwhelmed with emotion, I pulled the car over to the side of the road and penned these words:

> Your life with all its suffering has been hard to understand,
> But I know my heavenly Father has cradled you in His hand.
> He's the source of my strength and upholds me when His plan I cannot see.
> I don't need to understand when I know you're in my Father's hand.
> You're my Father's son, I can place you in His hand.
> His plan for you is greater than I'll ever understand.
> Though the journey that's unfolded has brought pain, beloved one,
> I won't fear tomorrow because I know…you're my Father's son.
> When life with all its trials presses in on every side,
> You're weary and discouraged by every attempt you've tried.
> Remember, God's almighty hand is sifting with great care.
> His loving hand is under you, and He knows what you can bear.

(Austin's verse)

I'm the Father's son, He will keep me in His hand.

His plan for me is greater than I'll ever understand.

The journey that's unfolded has brought pain,

I won't fear tomorrow because I know…I'm the Father's son.

Those words became a song titled "Our Father's Son," which our family sang to one audience after another. But the real import of it was what it meant to me and to Austin. It reinforced God's promises to be claimed. It served as a reminder that a sovereign God was always there, and I could entrust my son and my future into his hands even if that meant Austin would not recover.

This truth was a long time coming. I had been taught that we are to surrender our lives to God, and I did so at a young age. And as a Christian adult, I remained surrendered to God—at least to a point.

But when you do not receive answers to your prayers—at least not to your satisfaction—it's easy to try to take control of your own circumstances. I asked God to heal Austin and take away his pain. And when his pain persisted, I stepped in to try to relieve it myself. That's natural. I suppose I subconsciously thought, *If God's not going to step in and control this situation, then I will.* But on the day I penned the words to "My Father's Son," the idea of God's control took on a whole new meaning.

I sensed that God was calling me to hold on to a trust in him that he would care for Austin. He was calling me to trust him with my future, even if that future included pain, suffering, and the eventual death of my son. The apostle Peter said that Jesus was also called to entrust his future into his Father's hands, even if that meant pain, suffering, and his eventual death. And we are to follow his example.

> God called you to do good, even if it means suffering, just as Christ suffered for you. He is your example, and you must follow in his steps.
>
> He never sinned, nor ever deceived anyone. He did not retaliate when he was insulted, nor threaten revenge when he suffered. He left

his case [entrusted himself] in the hands of God, who always judges
fairly. (1 Peter 2:21–23)

Here are Jesus' last words on the cross: "'Father, I entrust my spirit into your hands!'
And with those words he breathed his last" (Luke 23:46). Jesus' trust in his Father's hands
did not disappoint. Because Jesus was the perfect and sinless sacrifice, death had no hold on
him. He rose victorious over death and became our hope of salvation, which includes the
forgiveness of sin and life eternal. That means one day he will correct all the injustices in the
world and do away with all suffering.

"Now we live with great expectation, and we have a priceless inheritance—an inheritance that is kept in heaven for you" (1 Peter 1:3–4). That "priceless inheritance" involves us
being "transformed into bodies that will never die" (1 Corinthians 15:53). This is a promised time when death will be "swallowed up in victory" (v. 54), and when we will live with
our loved ones in a beautiful place where "there will be no more death or sorrow or crying
or pain" (Revelation 21:4).

God wanted me to understand that he was ultimately in control. He wanted me to see
his eternal plan and claim his promise to reunite our family with Austin in heaven for all
eternity. But more than that, he wanted me to know he would take care of me and my family
right here on earth in spite of our dire circumstances. He was still in control and had a plan
for our lives even though our suffering here on earth seemed so senseless and unfair. He was
beginning to get through to me. I began to realize that just as he entrusted himself and his
future into the hands of his Father, I was to be like him and do the same. He wanted me to
live a life of holding on to my faith in him and trust myself to his good hands. That was the
prophet Habakkuk's message to Israel during their suffering. God told Habakkuk:

This vision is for a future time. It describes the end, and it will be fulfilled. If it seems slow in coming, wait patiently, for it will surely take
place. It will not be delayed. Look at the proud! They trust in themselves, and their lives are crooked. But the righteous will live by their
faithfulness to God. (Habakkuk 2:3–4)

There it was. God wanted me to live a life of holding on to my faith in him even though our present situation felt unfair and even though I couldn't see any plan that made any sense to me. "When troubles of any kind come your way," James wrote, "consider it an opportunity for great joy. For you know that when your faith is tested, your endurance has a chance to grow" (James 1:2–3).

When great suffering comes your way, it may feel as though everything is out of control, and you may not be able to make sense of it all. Know then that your faith is being tested. God wants you to rest in his hands and resist the temptation to control your own destiny.

What our family had to do is what I think all of us that suffer loss must do:

> *Let go* of the unproductive perspective that we control our own destiny, and *hold on* to our trust that God has our present and eternal future in his hands.

The prayer of King David can become the prayer of each of us who is suffering a loss. Make this prayer your own and every day claim the promise that the Lord "is gracious in all he does. The Lord helps the fallen and lifts those bent beneath their loads" (Psalm 145:13–14).

The Psalmist's Prayer

> I entrust my spirit into your hand. Rescue me, Lord, for you are a faithful God.
>
> My body and soul are withering away. I am dying from grief; my years are shortened by sadness.
>
> But I am trusting you, O Lord, saying, "You are my God!" My future is in your hands. (31:5, 9–10, 14–15)

It has been years since Austin's passing, and still there are days when I feel the pain of my loss. I still miss him, and I always will in this earthly life. In those moments of recurring grief, I entrust him again into God's hands. And God reassures me he is safe and that he is taking great care of Austin—my son and *his* son! That gives me great peace of mind.

ASSIGNMENT

A Matter of Trust

You and your journey partner can work through this exercise together, or you can complete it on your own and share it with him or her when you meet together.

You have no doubt endured much suffering. There is no easy way to grieve. It hurts and it drains you. Yet, in spite of the grief, there are things you and I can be thankful for. When we take a moment to focus on those for which we can be thankful, it helps us to gain a new perspective.

Think about what there is to be thankful for even though you are still grieving. Write out what you are still grateful for here.

Thank you, Lord for reminding me of the blessings I can be grateful for even during this time. Today, I'm especially thankful for...

Read these expressions of gratitude aloud with your partner.

It is not necessarily easy to hold on to a trust that your future is in God's hands. There are often feelings of uncertainty and fear surrounding any of life's losses. But one thing that helps is to know people are praying for you, particularly one person.

Just prior to the apostle Peter's denial of Jesus, someone told him they were praying for him. That someone was Jesus. "Simon, Simon," Jesus said to Peter, "Satan has asked to sift each of you like wheat. But I have pleaded in prayer for you, Simon, that your faith should not fail" (Luke 22:31–32).

When you stop to think about it, that is amazing. The Son of God, the Sovereign Lord of the universe, took the time to pray specifically for Peter. But what is even more amazing is that Jesus doesn't just pray for people named Peter. He is praying for you as you go through your suffering.

ENGAGE IN FELLOWSHIP

But when I am afraid, I will put my trust in you.
PSALM 56:3

The apostle John tells us: "There is someone to plead for you before the Father. He is Jesus Christ, the one...who pleases God completely" (1 John 2:1 TLB). And the Holy Spirit joins in those prayers for you so intensely that Scripture says his groaning "cannot be expressed in words" (Romans 8:26).

How do you respond to the truth that Jesus is praying specifically for you? How does that make you feel? Write out your words of gratefulness to Jesus for his prayers for you.

When I reflect on Jesus' prayers for me during this time, it moves my heart with...

Share these prayers with your partner. Celebrate the gratitude you feel.

These three things are certain:

- First, God cares for you both now and in your future.

- Second, he cares for both your loved one and you!

- Third, Jesus is praying for you.

Knowing these three certainties, can you now entrust to him your present and future life?

Tell God how you want to hold on to trusting your future to him. Express to him any fears you might have, and ask him to give you the courage to entrust your current and future life to him. He is worthy of your trust. Write out your prayer expressing your desire to trust your life and future to him.

God, even though there are times when I'm afraid of…

I am putting my trust in you…

Read your prayer aloud to your partner.

Partner: Pray words of strength and encouragement with your friend that he or she will hold on to this trust in God and keep entrusting the present and future into his hands.

Here is a prayer of the apostle Paul that you can take to heart:

> I pray that from his glorious, unlimited resources he will empower you with inner strength through his Spirit. Then Christ will make his home in your hearts as you trust in him. Your roots will grow down into God's love and keep you strong. And may you have the power to understand, as all God's people should, how wide, how long, how high, and how deep his love is. May you experience the love of Christ, though it is too great to understand fully. Then you will be made complete with all the fullness of life and power that comes from God. (Ephesians 3:16–19)

 M2. A Spirit-empowered disciple lives with reverence and awe as God's Word becomes real in life, vocation, and calling.

ENCOUNTER JESUS

When Jesus saw him lying there, he knew that the man had been crippled for a long time. So Jesus said to him, "Do you truly long to be healed?"
JOHN 5:6 TPT

Scripture tells us there was a paralyzed man in Bethesda lying near a pool of water. He was a nobody in a beautiful place—a place where God's Spirit stirred the waters once a day with healing powers. The first person to step into the pool after this stirring would be healed. Because the man could not walk, he was never able to be the first into the pool. Healing and hope eluded him.

This is where we find Jesus—in places where human need requires divine intervention. The Savior stood over the man and asked. "Excuse me, sir, but do you truly long to be healed?" There was no demand, only the most honest question one could ask. "Do you want the impossible? Do you want the improbable? Are you ready to have your life changed?"

Take a moment to have your own personal encounter with Jesus. Listen as he asks the same questions of you, *What do you want me to do?* Tell him now, and he promises to take it and place it before the Father.

Next, move toward the place you desire to be. Jesus told the man, "Get up!" So now in your own way, speak up with gratitude. Take a step of vulnerability or action that demonstrates your faith.

> *Jesus, thank you that you hear me and that I can trust you for my future! I receive by faith the promise and power of your Holy Spirit to remove my fear and empower my faith. You have met me beside these troubled waters, and now I give you praise.*

 L10. A Spirit-empowered disciple practices the presence of the Lord, yielding to the Spirit's work of Christlikeness.

SECTION THREE

There Is a Purpose
God Wants to Reveal

11

For What Purpose?

This cold November morning was the worst day of our family's life. I (Duane) pulled Cindy and the children close together as we huddled under the canopy at the side of the open grave. Scripture had been read, and Austin's body was committed to the ground, "Ashes to ashes, dust to dust."

All our friends and other family members stood with us as the casket was being lowered into the ground. Quiet sobs could be heard as some softly sang hymns about heaven. Then, one by one, those with us took turns gently shoveling dirt into the open grave.

Soon a mound of dirt adorned the place where a son and brother lay. Flowers were placed upon the dirt, and we said our final goodbye.

The finality of it all felt surreal. Yet I tried to be reassuring to Cindy and the girls with the thought that we would one day be reunited with Austin. But the futuristic thought of seeing him again was overshadowed by the pain of the moment—especially the pain of betrayal.

Our daughter Brianna was fourteen years old at the time. She, along with all of us, had been so hopeful after Austin's second heart transplant. We felt God had answered our prayers for Austin's full recovery. But now this.

Brianna shared her struggles with us. "I prayed for Austin and trusted God," she said. "And God gave him a new heart. Austin was doing so well. Then this happened. How can I ever trust God again? I feel so betrayed!"

I had no logical answer. Logic wouldn't have helped anyway. It was what it was. God had not intervened.

Not Just Going through It but Also Growing through It

After Austin's death, numerous people told us God was ultimately in control and that he was working out his purpose and that good would come out of this. They quoted Paul's well-known words, "God causes everything to work together for the good of those who love God and are called according to his purpose for them" (Romans 8:28).

At the time, that was not of much comfort to me or my family. Good and purpose were the furthest from our minds or emotions. We could see nothing resulting from our ordeal except pain and suffering.

I'm the first to say that I don't understand why God chooses to intervene in some situations and not in others. His ways are clearly mysterious. God makes that clear in Scripture. "'My thoughts are nothing like your thoughts,' says the Lord. 'And my ways are far beyond anything you could imagine'" (Isaiah 55:8). The apostle Paul put it this way: "Oh, how great are God's riches and wisdom and knowledge! How impossible it is for us to understand his decisions and his ways!" (Romans 11:33).

One of my problems was that I had not fully understood the promise of Romans 8:28. First, God's Word doesn't say our trials, loss, and suffering are good. There is certainly nothing good about death from a griever's perspective.

However, what this verse is telling us is the good that God is working out is ultimately for our benefit. God is causing everything, both good and bad, to work together. And it is working together for *the good of us* who love him and are called according to *his purpose for us*.

God desires that we not only go through our suffering—that we endure it—but also that we grow through it. This growth is for our good, and it is a good that we could not have achieved except through suffering. Paul defines the good in the very next verse. "For God knew his people in advance, and he chose them to become like his Son" (Romans 8:29). In other words, God is causing everything that does happen to us—both bad and good—to work together in order that we might grow to become more and more like him.

It doesn't matter if everything that comes our way is good; God is weaving the tragic things together with his purposes so that we can grow to be more like Christ. Why is God obsessed with us being like his Son? Because as we reflect the image of God in which he created us, it gives us both meaning and joy. And experiencing meaning and joy in life is very good.

Jesus said, "I have told you this so that my joy may be in you and that your joy may be complete" (John 15:11 NIV). That is what God wants for us, to grow to be like his Son so we can experience maximum joy as we fulfill his calling on our life. And what does that do for God? It gives *him* joy.

"Even before he made the world," Paul wrote, "God loved us and chose us in Christ to be holy" (Ephesians 1:4). To be holy is to be like his Son. God's unchanging plan has always been to adopt us into his own family. And what does this do? "It gave him great pleasure" (v. 5).

When we grow to be more like Christ, it does give God "great pleasure." But it also reflects honorably and well on him—it gives him glory. That is the other purpose God has in mind in "causing everything to work together for good." He wants to receive glory out of our lives. "For everything comes from him and exists by his power and is intended for his glory" (Romans 11:36).

So there it is—God is causing everything, both the good and the not-so-good to work out for our good and his glory, especially as our growth in Christlikeness points others to Jesus. He can use struggles in our lives to refine and redefine us for the good. And he is particularly adept at bringing good out of our weak and shattered lives.

He Makes Beautiful Things Out of Dust

Did our tragedy break us to the point that we didn't know how we could go on? Yes, but God has a way of making broken things beautiful. It takes broken soil to produce beautiful flowers. Broken clouds give refreshing rain. Broken grain yields life-giving bread.

It is in the shattered moments of life that God wants to reveal his heart of love and restoration for the purpose of our good and his glory. He accomplishes this feat by making beautiful things out of the crumbling dust of our lives.

In fact, songwriter Michael Gungor caught a glimpse of the God who makes beautiful things out of dust when he penned the lyrics to his song, "Beautiful Things."

As a couple and a family, we prayed that God would take the broken pieces of our lives wrought by pain—the dust—and make a beautiful thing. God wanted to lift us up out of despair and heartbrokenness, provide for our good, and receive glory out of even the worst of our circumstances. And he did.

Remember Jesus words? "Here on this earth you will have many trials and sorrow. But take heart, because I have overcome the world" (John 16:33). God took Jesus' horrific suffering and death and made a beautiful thing—a means to have eternal life. God received glory out of the worst travesty of all time, the death of the sinless Son of God. And he wants to receive glory out of our travesties as well.

God has been doing that for his people down through the ages. He overcame the barrenness of Sarah, Abraham's wife, and raised up the nation of Israel through the birth of Isaac. He freed his people out of slavery in Egypt, opened up the Red Sea, and led them to the land he had promised them. He took the tragedy of a weakened and blinded Samson and brought destruction to the wicked Philistines. He brought victory over the giant Goliath through a young man named David, who had no military training—just a sling and a stone. There was Daniel, who survived the lion's den, the three Hebrew boys who overcame the fiery furnace, and many more.

Perhaps the story that best reveals God's masterful transforming of losses into victories is that of Joseph. God worked through several evil circumstances—Joseph being sold into slavery by his jealous brothers and imprisoned unjustly by an Egyptian official—to elevate him to the position of prime minister over the entire nation of Egypt. Through Joseph's leadership, God led Egypt through a terrible famine. When Joseph's brothers who had sold him into slavery years before came to Egypt to buy food, Joseph told them, "God turned into good what you meant for evil" (Genesis 50:20 TLB). Through the misfortune and tragedy Joseph suffered, God worked things out for Joseph's good and God's glory.

God has demonstrated over and over that he is in the business of transforming tragedy into triumph. He doesn't want our pain to become our prison. Even in our darkest hours, God wants to reveal, not a purpose for our pain, but a renewed purpose for us—a renewed purpose of good that gives God honor and glory out of our broken and shattered lives.

So we encourage you to:

> *Let go* **of your past normal, offer God your present broken and shat-tered life, and** *hold on* **to your new normal and renewed purpose that God will reveal.**

We don't simply let go of our broken, shattered, and painful life; we give it away to God as a living sacrifice. And we do this not once but day by day. Then we can pray:

> Lord, each day take my crumbled life, my broken spirit and sorrowing soul and raise it up for my good and your glory. I seek to bring honor to you each day by becoming more and more like you. As I follow you, "give a crown of beauty for ashes, a joyous blessing instead of mourn-ing, festive praise instead of despair." (Isaiah 61:3)

King David prayed a similar prayer after he turned away from his bitterness.

> I realized my heart was bitter, and I was all torn up inside. I was so foolish and ignorant...Yet I still belong to you; you hold my right hand. You guide me with your counsel, leading me to a glorious des-tiny. (Psalm 73:21–24)

You belong to God too. He holds your right hand as well. And he will lead you step-by-step to a glorious destiny. He doesn't expect you to achieve this destiny on your own, by your own strength. In fact, the opposite is true. Your good and his glory are best accomplished through your weakness.

God's Power Works Best in Weakness

The apostle Paul went through a lot of suffering. He dealt continually with one unnamed problem that tormented him relentlessly. He asked God repeatedly to take the painful thing away. But Paul said God told him, "My grace is all you need. My power works best in weakness." Paul went on to say, "So now I am glad to boast about my weaknesses, so that the power of Christ can work through me…For when I am weak, then I am strong" (2 Corinthians 12:9–10).

The power of Christ works best through our weakness, brokenness, and shattered lives so that he gets the glory, not us. You and I can become a conduit of God's power to minister to others. We can be a conduit of comfort to others because we ourselves have been comforted. As Paul said, "He comforts us in our troubles so that we can comfort others. When they are troubled, we will be able to give them the same comfort God has given us" (1:4).

Being a conduit of God's comfort to others is where our own family first began to see God getting glory out of our loss. Whenever we met someone who was grieving a loss, we could empathize—even if their loss was something other than a loved one. We were able to relate and minister to anyone who was suffering a loss, whether it was a relational breakup, a divorce, a loss of property, or abuse as a child or an adult. It wasn't that we became professional counselors. We simply could feel the pain of their loss because we had been there too. And because we had received comfort, we could give comfort—the same comfort God had given us.

Through it all we found a renewed sense of purpose. God took our experience with suffering and death and transformed it into a "Pain 2 Purpose" ministry to others. In addition to the seminars we conduct, we regularly meet with prison inmates. We sing to them, share our story, and minister comfort to their wounded souls.

You may not engage in a traveling ministry like ours, but God wants to miraculously work out your circumstances for your good and his glory. Depending on how far along you are on your grief journey, you may even sense that now you are far more empathetic to those who are suffering a loss. That means you are becoming experientially qualified to provide godlike comfort to those in emotional pain. This is an indication that you are being given a renewed purpose—to give God glory by comforting others with the comfort he has given you. And that is extremely rewarding.

That means, out of the soil of your weakness and brokenness blossoms glory to God. God said, "My power works best in weakness" (12:9). Even as you are grieving your own loss, God can empower you to connect and relate to other people's losses just like he does. It is then that his comfort flows through you to bring healing comfort to a hurting soul. In a real sense, you become a partner with God in his ministry of comfort. Think of it: God considers you a part of his ministry and mission in the world!

As God begins to work and minister through you, it does not go unnoticed. He does get the glory because people recognize that your ministry to them is authentic because he has ministered to you. Paul said, "This light and power that now shines within us—is held in a perishable container, that is, in our weak bodies. Everyone can see that the glorious power within must be from God and is not our own" (4:7 TLB).

God can give us the strength to let go of our false or real guilt, our regrets, fears, anger, sense of unworthiness or sense of control, and even our past normal. He can give us the strength to hold on to healing comfort, the freedom of forgiveness, the belief that God is good, that he is with us, and to the trust that our present and future is in his hands. As we continually let go and hold on, God can do a supernatural work in our lives each day. We become "mirrors that brightly reflect the glory of the Lord. And as the Spirit of the Lord works within us, we become more and more like him" (3:18 TLB).

For what purpose do we suffer? There may not be a revealed purpose for the pain and suffering you are going through, but there can be a revealed purpose for *you*. That purpose is to reflect God's glory even more! When you continue to look to him and entrust your future to him each day, you will receive joy, and he will receive glory. "The Lord says, 'I will guide you along the best pathway for your life. I will advise you and watch over you'" (Psalm 32:8). As you do this, he becomes your strength, and you become his shining witness. "My life is an example to many, because you have been my strength and protection. That is why I can never stop praising you; I declare your glory all day long" (71:7–8).

EXPERIENCE SCRIPTURE

Surely your goodness and unfailing love will pursue me all the days of my life.

PSALM 23:6

Psalm 23 is a familiar and often-quoted passage of Scripture. It's filled with messages of comfort and reminders of how God is our Good Shepherd. The psalmist also reminds us that when we walk through the darkest valleys of life, our Shepherd is with us and very near to us.

The last verse of the psalm reveals another important truth on our journey through the valleys of life. Not only are we told that the Lord is with us but also that his goodness and his unfailing love will pursue us. In other words, it's as if God's goodness and love are chasing after us, hoping to catch us so we can experience more and more of the Shepherd's care!

Here's our dilemma: In order for God's goodness, unfailing love, and his revealed purpose to catch up to us, we have to be still. When we're still before the Lord, we experience more of our good God (Psalm 46:10). Let's try that now.

Spend the next few moments being still. Find a quiet place. Quiet your mind and your heart. Pray the prayers below and then listen for God's response.

Because you are a God of love, I know that your goodness and your love are trying to catch me. Here I am, God. I want to be still so I can better hear you and know you (Psalm 46:10). Lord, would you reveal some of the good purposes you have for me and my journey? Would you begin to reveal how my journey might enable me to give you glory? Make me a witness of your love and compassion. Grant me your confident peace and expectant hope.

 M6. A Spirit-empowered disciple bears witness of a confident peace and expectant hope in God's lordship in all things.

12

Goodbye and Hello

How many times have you said goodbye in your lifetime? Probably as many times as you have said hello. It's a pattern. You and I meet people and depart from them. We arrive somewhere and then leave. We spend a season of time with family and friends, then that season ends, and we say goodbye to the old and hello to the new.

Life is a series of seasons. Preschool childhood is a season of life. Then comes elementary school life, high school, and college. There is a season of being single that can last a lifetime for some. There are those who have a season of being married. A season of life can be related to a career, having and raising children, becoming empty nesters, moving to a new area, and retirement.

As we move through each season of life, we consciously or subconsciously should be saying goodbye to the old (letting go) and hello to the new (holding on). If only it were that simple! Many times we fail to make clean breaks from our past. Consequently, we carry painful emotions from the previous season of life into the next.

Throughout much of our journey through this book, we have attempted to guide you through a process of letting go or saying goodbye to certain unproductive things (e.g., guilt, regrets, fears, anger, resentments, a sense of unworthiness, or self-reliance, etc.). Those things are an unproductive mix of burdens that can load you down and hinder you from saying hello to your future new normal. You have been encouraged to say hello or to hold on to healing comfort, forgiveness, freedom from fear, renewed trust in God, spiritual strength, a greater sense of wholeness, and emotional peace of mind.

There may be other goodbyes and hellos you may need to experience, but this last one is perhaps the most difficult as it relates to the loss of your loved one. It is saying goodbye to your past normal. It is letting go of the season of life you had with your loved one. And that is extremely difficult.

This letting go doesn't mean we are saying goodbye to our love, devotion, and memories of the ones we lost. We will never do that, nor should we. We should hold on dearly to the precious things our loved ones gave to us when they were alive. We may have deeply implanted in our memories their tender face of compassion, the unique sound of their laughter, their quirky sense of humor, or their courage in the face of suffering. The personal qualities of what made them unique individuals can and should be held on to and never let go. However, the season of life that included their physical presence is past. So if we are to live a meaningful life on this earth in the present, we must now live it without experiencing a personal relationship with them.

You may not yet be in the place where you can do this. There is so much to adjust to in saying goodbye to your past normal with your loved one, especially if that person was a significant part of your everyday life. But your journey to a new normal can slowly and steadily become a reality as you continually let go of the unproductive grief and hold on to those things that we have covered thus far in this book.

Assessing Your Progress

It can be a source of encouragement to realize you are making progress in letting go and holding on. Little things can be indicators. You may be eating and sleeping better. You may be getting out more, crying less, laughing on occasion, remembering your loved one with a measure of fondness without intense pain, or reaching other small but significant goals. These are indicators that you are beginning to adjust, and that should be a source of encouragement to you.

That last indicator noted above—memories that produce fondness rather than intense pain—is a major one, for it shows that you are, in fact, making significant progress. When memories of your loved one begin to be pleasant rather than flooded with grief, it means you are beginning to separate your love from your loss. As you unburden yourself of the unproductive grief you may be carrying, pleasant memories of your loved one can outweigh the pain of the loss. That is when your new normal begins to be tolerable. Though it may be hard to imagine it now, that new normal can eventually grow into a life full of joy. You will always miss your loved one, but that doesn't mean you miss out on a future life of happiness. Don't be discouraged if you are not there yet. Be patient and avoid putting pressure on yourself if you're not as far along as you hoped. It is a long journey.

ASSIGNMENT

Sharing My Progress

To assess your progress thus far, reflect on these factors and discuss them with your journey partner.

- **Receiving Comfort**

Comfort is medicine for a broken heart. Have you been able to meaningfully accept comfort from your partner and others? Or have you struggled to allow that comfort to sink deep into your emotions?

A sense of unworthiness and self-reliance have been identified as obstacles to meaningfully receiving comfort. Simply expressing words of thanks can help you truly receive another's comfort and compassion. To what degree have you been able to overcome those obstacles and hold on to the healing power of comfort for the loss of your loved one?

Write out your assessment of how well you receive comfort.

• Backlog of Hurts

We have noted that unresolved pain in our past will complicate the recovery process. Failing to address major hurts in our past compounds the hurts in our present. Have you been able to uncover some past hurts and find a measure of healing comfort for them? To what degree has that lifted a burden that had prevented you from receiving comfort for your recent loss?

Write out your assessment on how well you have received comfort for past hurts.

• Questioning God

There are few satisfying answers as to why we suffer and why God allows it to go on. Have you struggled with unanswered questions yet still maintained your faith in a good and merciful God? Have you moved on from asking why to asking a new question: Does God care? Have you been able to experience the joy and gratitude that comes from deeply knowing God's care for you? In times of suffering, it can be difficult to claim his promises that he is your shelter, strength, and refuge. How are you progressing in this area?

Write out your assessment of how you have or have not been able to maintain spiritual strength.

• "Guilt" and Regrets

It is nearly impossible to lose someone close and not struggle with some feelings of guilt (those if-onlys) and regrets (those not-enoughs). It just seems that someone or something is to blame, and we often point a finger at ourselves. Have you been able to identify some of your own guilt (false guilt) and regrets and yet find a measure of freedom and healing because you've embraced the truth that there is no condemnation for those who are in Christ Jesus (Romans 8:1)? Especially, have you been able to forgive yourself?

Write out your assessment on how well you have found a measure of freedom from guilt and regrets.

- **Resolving Unfinished Business**

As we indicated before, all relationships have their ups and downs. No human relationship is perfect. So it is probable that when you lost your loved one, there were some issues not fully resolved. Do you sense that, as a result of addressing some of those issues in your freedom and forgiveness work, you have brought a greater sense of completion to that relationship? How have you taken steps toward claiming God's promise of forgiveness and healing as you confess and forgive (1 John 1:9, Matthew 6:14)?

Write out your assessment on how successfully you may have brought about a greater sense of relational completion.

- ## **Anxiety and Fear**

After a major loss, it's natural to feel a measure of anxiety and fear about the future. Life can become uncertain, unknown, unfamiliar, and out of control. As a result, we may double down on trying to take control of our lives in an unhealthy way or look to others for some solution. Your own faith in a sovereign God may have been tested, making it difficult to entrust your future to his hands, but fully embracing his perfect love drives out our fear and frees us to trust again (1 John 4:18–19).

Write out an assessment of how well you have entrusted your life and future in the hands of God.

- ## **Goodbye and Hello**

It is not easy to say goodbye to your past normal and hello to a new normal that must be lived without your loved one. A beginning step is to offer your present broken and shattered life to God, who makes beautiful things out of dust. He is in the process of working out your situation for your good and his glory. For instance, he may have begun to move your heart with a deeper compassion and given you a greater ability to comfort others. God may be giving you the strength to talk to others about your loved one without being overcome with grief. These are just some of the ways God may be making beautiful things.

Write out an assessment of your progress in offering your broken heart and life of suffering to God and to what extent your good and God's glory are starting to be realized. Note: It may be too early in the process for you to be realizing this. Just share where you are in the process.

Your journey is in process. It is not over. You will continually need to receive comfort for your broken heart and wounded spirit. As your feelings of guilt and regrets emerge, you will repeatedly need to submit them before God to receive his assurances of acceptance and forgiveness. Your faith will continue to be tested, and entrusting your future into God's hands will be a repeated exercise.

Those of us who are on this journey need patience, especially patience with ourselves. God has begun a good work of recovery within us, and it continues. We are like those in the early church that the apostle Paul addressed: "I am certain that God, who began the good work within you, will continue his work until it is finally finished" (Philippians 1:6).

Continue on in your journey of grief. Continually unload yourself of unproductive grief and hold on to those productive and positive things that will help you move forward. As you do this, you will slowly but surely find your new normal. We pray that in time and by God's grace you will be able to embrace the prophetic words of Isaiah: "The Lord will be your everlasting light. Your days of mourning will come to an end" (Isaiah 60:20).

ENGAGE IN FELLOWSHIP

Come and listen, all you who fear God,
and I will tell you what he did for me.
PSALM 66:16

If you have completed the exercises in Chapter 12, you have the bulk of this Experiential completed. This is a time to share your overall progress with your partner. You may want to complete the written portions before meeting with your partner.

> *To the partner: Your friend has made progress. Yet the present stage is much nearer the beginning than the end. He or she will need your continual comfort, encouragement, and support. Let your friend know that you will be there throughout this journey—a journey from pain to a renewed purpose in life.*

As you share your progress, do not feel any pressure or sense that you are being examined or tested. There is no standard for you to measure up to or grade you are expected to achieve. You will not be judged.

Your progress is *your* progress. Share it openly and honestly. It will be freeing to share where you are in your journey, and it will allow your partner to both rejoice with you and know how better to journey with you.

- *My progress in receiving healing comfort*

(Share verbally what you wrote in Chapter 12 on "Receiving Comfort" or rewrite it here.)

- *My progress in finding added comfort for past pain (other than the pain caused by the recent loss of my loved one)*

(Share verbally what you wrote in Chapter 12 on "Backlog of Hurts" or rewrite it here.)

- *My progress on my feelings toward God and my spiritual strength*

(Share verbally what you wrote in Chapter 12 on "Questioning God" or rewrite it here.)

- *My progress on dealing with my guilt and regrets*

(Share verbally what you wrote in Chapter 12 on "Guilt and Regrets" or rewrite it here.)

- *My progress on resolving unfinished business with my lost loved one*

(Share verbally what you wrote in Chapter 12 on "Resolving Unfinished Business" or rewrite it here.)

- *My progress on dealing with any anxiety and fears I might have*

(Share verbally what you wrote in Chapter 12 on "Anxiety and Fear" or rewrite it here.)

- *My progress on saying goodbye to my past normal and hello to my new normal*

(Share verbally what you wrote in Chapter 12 on "Goodbye and Hello" or rewrite it here.)

 W4.   A Spirit-empowered disciple humbly and vulnerably shares of the Spirit's transforming work through the Word.

If you have gotten this far, you have almost completed this book. Yet, as we have said, your grief journey is far from over. Continue the process of letting go of those unproductive aspects of grief and continue to hold on to comfort for your past losses. Continue to hold on to God's promises in the present. And continue to anticipate and then hold on to a renewed purpose to be revealed in the future. There is hope, healing, and a life full of joy for you in the future.

Thank you for the opportunity to share our journey with you. In closing we offer this prayer for you:

Dear Lord, we thank you for your child who is on this grief journey. We know that this person is precious to you and will receive a lavish outpouring of your love and care. We pray that you will impart a special revelation of yourself. Grant this suffering child an awareness of your presence and the knowledge that it will continue throughout the process of healing. Guide this child in casting off the burden of unproductive grief and into a new normal filled again with joy. And in the process may you be honored, lifted up, and glorified. In the sweet name of Jesus. Amen.

"I have told you these things so that you will be filled with joy. Yes, your joy will overflow!" (John 15:11)

For a final experience in your *Pain 2 Purpose* journey, make these words of Jesus very personal. Spend the next moments encountering Jesus once more. Hear his prayers and his promises just for you.

ENCOUNTER JESUS

Jesus wants you to experience an unwavering trust in him and his Word. Listen to each of these verses and imagine the Savior sitting next to you. His eyes are full of compassion and hope. His voice is gentle and reassuring. Jesus' only agenda is sharing encouragement with you!

- I will be with you day after day after day, right up to the end of the age.

- *"And surely I am with you always, to the very end of the age"* (Matthew 28:20 NIV).

- I want my joy to be your joy and your joy to be wholly mature!

- *"I have told you this so that my joy may be in you and that your joy may be complete"* (John 15:11 NIV).

- Ask yourself what you want people to do for you; then grab the initiative and do it for them! You'll never regret it—I promise!

- *"Do to others as you would have them do to you…Then your reward will be great"* (Luke 6:31, 35 NIV).

- By opening up to others about your journey with me, you'll prompt people to open up with God.

- *"In the same way, let your light shine before others, that they may see your good deeds and glorify your Father in heaven"* (Matthew 5:16 NIV).

- In trusting me, you will be unshakable and assured, deeply at peace. In this godless world, you will continue to experience difficulties. But take heart! I've conquered the world.

- *"I have told you these things, so that in me you may have peace. In this world you will have trouble. But take heart! I have overcome the world"* (John 16:33 NIV).

Pause to consider how these verses bring more hope to your journey. Embrace these promises and thank God that he notices, prays, cares, and encourages you with his Word!

Spend your final moments thanking Christ for sharing these promises and prayers with you. Tell him about your gratitude. Give him your praise.

God, in the final moments of this journey, I want to declare my praise for you. I am grateful that you have been my guide because…

I praise you for being a God who…

 W7.   A Spirit-empowered disciple's life is explained as one of "experiencing Scripture."

SECTION FOUR

Other Losses

13

The Journey of Recovery from Other Losses

This book has focused primarily on recovering from loss due to the death of a loved one. However, the grief recovery process is applicable to other losses as well.

You may have suffered the loss of a job, a loss of a relationship, the loss of property as a result of a natural disaster, the loss of health, or the loss of a sense of worth or personhood due to sexual abuse. These are major losses, and you will need time to grieve and heal emotionally.

The process we have described and applied in the previous chapters is equally valid for recovery from these five additional losses. We offer the following guidelines in dealing with these losses.

Loss of a Job

Being laid off or fired from a job can be emotionally and financially devastating. This situation can greatly impact your self-esteem, social standing, and sense of security. Even if you have found a new job, the effect of losing your previous job may have left you emotionally wounded, and in varying degrees, you need healing of a broken heart, renewed spiritual strength, a renewed sense of wholeness, emotional peace of mind, and a renewed sense of purpose. Like those who suffer the loss of a loved one, you, too, need to move forward in life and find a new normal.

We suggest that you read through this book with a friend who will act as your journey partner. Together the two of you will complete the exercises and apply them to your specific loss.

Your Need for Comfort

Whether your job loss has hurt you minimally or left you with a major emotional wound, you need comfort. Finish your reading of Chapter 2, go on to read Chapter 3, and then complete the exercises there. Apply these truths to your own situation and receive needed comfort from God.

A Backlog of Hurts

After reading Chapter 4, complete the Assignment: "A Chart of Past Hurts." Be sure to include any past hurts related to how your parent's job choices affected you, any job conflicts you experienced as a young person, and struggles early in your career up to your current job loss. Mourn those losses—as well as your current loss—with your journey partner and openly receive comfort from him or her.

God Cares

God cares about what is happening in your life right now. You may have questions as to why you have to be suffering through your current circumstances, yet God cares and hurts with you. Read Chapter 5 and complete the Assignment: "Can You Hear Me Now?" and apply it all to your situation.

A Letter of Freedom and Forgiveness

You may very well be struggling with regrets, guilt, resentment, assigning blame, and other difficult emotions. While you may not be missing a loved one, you may be missing your old routine, your colleagues, your previous social network, and the satisfaction and economic security your job provided you. You may have emotions to process and some unresolved relationships with your former boss or company. Read Chapters 6–8 and complete the Assignments for freedom and forgiveness and apply those truths to your specific loss.

In Good Hands

A loss of a job can certainly affect one's sense of security. The future may feel uncertain, and you may be struggling to find emotional peace of mind. Read through Chapters 9–10, complete the Assignment: "A Matter of Trust," and apply those truths to your life.

For What Purpose?

There may not be an apparent purpose for the pain you are going through right now, but there is a renewed purpose for you. Read Chapters 11–12, complete the Assignment "Sharing My Progress" and apply it to your situation.

Helpful Resources

Letting go of an old job or career and moving forward to a new normal is challenging. Following are a few suggested resources designed to help you move forward.

Melinda Smith, Jeanne Segal, and Lawrence Robinson, "Job Loss and Unemployment Stress: Coping with the Stress of Losing a Job," Help Guide, April 2020, https://www.helpguide.org/articles/stress/job-loss-and-unemployment-stress.htm.

Al Siebert, "How to Handle the Emotional Side of Job Loss and Job Search with Resiliency," Al Siebert Resiliency Center, https://resiliencycenter.com/handle-the-emotional-side-of-job-loss-with-resiliency/.

Alan D. Wolfelt and Kirby J. Duvall, *Healing after Job Loss: 100 Practical Ideas* (Fort Collins, CO: Companion Press, 2011).

★ ★ ★ ★ ★

Loss of a Relationship Due to Divorce

Divorce can be as devastating as experiencing the death of a friend. Except in death, the person is gone from the earth. In a divorce, we experience the death of a love relationship, but the person is not gone physically. That fact alone may be challenging.

Whether or not you sought the divorce, you have suffered a loss that needs to be grieved. You have an old life with your ex that you need to let go of emotionally, and you need to move forward and find a new normal.

No doubt you have suffered emotional wounds and to varying degrees need healing for a broken heart, renewed spiritual strength, a renewed sense of wholeness, emotional peace of mind, and a renewed sense of purpose. That is what the grieving and recovery process described in this book is designed to help you accomplish. While this book has applied the recovery process primarily to the loss of a loved one, the truths are applicable to many other emotional losses, including the loss due to divorce. You also might want to seek counseling from someone who is experienced in helping those suffering from the losses that can result from divorce.

We suggest you read through this book with a friend who will act as your journey partner. Together you will complete the Experiential exercises and apply them to your specific loss.

Your Need for Comfort

The loss of a relationship is emotionally painful. The extent of the pain many vary based on the situation surrounding the breakup. But emotional wounds are real wounds, and they need to be healed. And that is where the healing ministry of comfort comes in.

Finish your reading of Chapter 2, and then go on to read Chapter 3, along with the Experiential exercises. As you read, apply the truths to your specific situation and receive needed comfort from God.

A Backlog of Hurts

After reading Chapter 4 complete the Assignment: "A Chart of Past Hurts." Be sure to include any past hurts related to relational breakups as a young person, relational tensions at home, and conflicts that negatively affected you. An example might be the breakup of your parents, your breakup with a girlfriend or boyfriend, or the departure of a good friend. Mourn those losses—as well as your current loss—with your journey partner and openly receive comfort from him or her.

God Cares

God cares about what is happening in your life right now. You may have questions as to why you have to suffer through your current circumstances, yet God cares and hurts with you. Read Chapter 5 and complete the Assignment "Can You Hear Me Now?" and then apply it all to your situation.

Freedom and Forgiveness

You may very well be struggling with regrets, guilt, resentment, and assigning blame. You may be missing your old routine and old friends. Your entire home environment may have changed, and your economic security may have been shaken. Undoubtedly, you have emotions to process and possibly some unresolved relationship issues that need healing.

Read Chapters 6–8 and complete the exercises for freedom and forgiveness as you apply those truths to your specific loss.

In Good Hands

A loss of a relationship can certainly affect one's sense of security. The future may feel uncertain, and you may struggle to find emotional peace of mind. Read through Chapters 9–10 and complete the Assignment "A Matter of Trust." Apply those truths to your life.

For What Purpose?

There may not be an apparent purpose for the pain you are going through right now, but there is a renewed purpose for you. Read Chapters 11–12 and complete the Assignment "Sharing My Progress," and then apply it to your situation.

Helpful Resources

Moving forward after a divorce is a challenge. Following are a few suggested resources designed to help you move forward to a new normal. Your church may have recovery groups and counseling you will want to take advantage of.

> Whitney Hopler, "16 Ways to Find Healing and Hope after Divorce," Crosswalk.com, April 6, 2005, https://www.crosswalk.com/family/marriage/find-healing-and-hope-after-divorce-1322747.html.

> Winston T. Smith, "Divorce Recovery: Practical Strategies for Change," Crosswalk.com, November 1, 2008, https://www.crosswalk.com/family/marriage/divorce-recovery-practical-strategies-for-change-11582907.html.

* * * * *

Loss Following a Natural Disaster

For centuries, natural disasters have wreaked havoc on life, property, and emotions. Tornados, hurricanes, floods, earthquakes, fire, and a multitude of other disasters have brought misery to many. You may have escaped physical injury, but the loss of meaningful possessions has no doubt taken an emotional toll.

It is not uncommon for those who have experienced loss as a result of a natural disaster to feel overwhelmed, confused, panic, anxiety, anger, guilt, and a heavy sense of grief. As a victim, you may have sustained deep emotional wounds, and you need healing of a broken heart, renewed spiritual strength, a renewed sense of wholeness, emotional peace of mind, and a renewed sense of purpose. Like those who are suffering the loss of a loved one, you, too, need to move forward in life and find a new normal.

We suggest that you read through this book with a friend who will act as your journey partner. Together you will complete the exercises and apply them to your specific loss.

Your Need for Comfort

Whether the loss of your property and/or personal possessions has hurt you minimally or left you with a major emotional wound, you need comfort. Finish your reading of Chapter 2, go on to read Chapter 3, and then complete the Experiential exercises. Apply these truths to your own situation and receive needed comfort from God.

A Backlog of Hurts

After reading Chapter 4, complete the Assignment: "A Chart of Past Hurts." Be sure to include any past hurts related to losses that were dear to you as a child or valuable items that were taken from you. Mourn those losses—as well as your current loss—with your journey partner and openly receive comfort from him or her.

God Cares

God cares about what is happening in your life right now. You may have questions as to why you have to be suffering through your circumstances, yet God cares and hurts with you. Read Chapter 5 and complete the Assignment "Can You Hear Me Now?" Apply it all to your situation.

Freedom and Forgiveness

You may very well be struggling with regrets, guilt, resentment, and assigning blame. While you may not be missing a loved one, you may be missing your home, your property, your old routine, and the satisfaction and economic security your possessions provided you. No doubt you have emotions to process and some unresolved relationships to deal with. Read Chapters 6–8, complete the exercises for freedom and forgiveness, and apply those truths to your specific loss.

In Good Hands

Losing a home and/or personal possessions can certainly affect one's sense of security. The future may feel uncertain, and you may be struggling with emotional peace of mind. Read through Chapters 9–10 and complete the Assignment "A Matter of Trust," then apply those truths to your life.

For What Purpose?

There may not be an apparent purpose for the pain you are going through right now, but there is a renewed purpose for you. Read Chapters 11–12 and complete the Assigment "Sharing My Progress." Then apply the material to your situation.

Helpful Resources

Letting go of all you have lost and moving forward to a new normal is challenging. Following are a few suggested resources designed to help you move forward.

> "Recovering Emotionally from Disaster," American Psychological Association, 2013, https://www.apa.org/topics/disasters-response/recovering.

> "Coping with Public Tragedies and Natural Disasters," VITAS Healthcare, https://www.vitas.com/family-and-caregiver-support/grief-and-bereavement/coping-with-grief/coping-with-public-tragedies-and-natural-disasters.

> Dr. Alan D. Wolfelt, *Healing Your Grief When Disaster Strikes* (Fort Collins, CO: Companion Press, 2014).

* * * * *

Loss of Physical Health

Whether you are suffering a temporary physical loss of health, a chronic or terminal illness, or have been physically impacted by the Covid-19 virus, you are suffering a major loss. Those losses can include the loss of comfort and joy, freedom of movement, independence, cognitive functions, income, self-esteem, self-control, hope, dignity, certainty, and security. The loss of health can take a tremendous toll on your emotional and spiritual well-being. You may have sustained deep emotional wounds and are in need of healing of a broken heart, renewed spiritual strength, a renewed sense of emotional wholeness, peace of mind, and a renewed sense of purpose. Like those who are suffering the loss of a loved one, you, too, need to move forward, even in a life of illness, to a new normal.

We suggest that you read through this book with a friend who will act as your journey partner. Together you will complete the Experiential exercises and apply them to your loss of physical health.

Your Need for Comfort

Loss of health is a significant loss that needs to be grieved and comforted. Finish your reading of Chapter 2, go on to read Chapter 3, and then complete the Assignments there. Apply these truths to your own situation and receive needed comfort from God.

A Backlog of Hurts

After reading Chapter 4, complete the Assignment "A Chart of Past Hurts." Be sure to include any past hurts related to a time you were sick or injured and couldn't be as active as your family and friends. Mourn those losses—as well as your current health loss—with your journey partner and openly receive comfort from him or her.

God Cares

God cares about what is happening in your life right now. You may have questions as to why you have to be suffering through your difficult circumstances, yet God cares and hurts with you. Read Chapter 5 and complete the Assignment "Can You Hear Me Now?" Then apply it all to your situation.

Freedom and Forgiveness

You may very well be struggling with regrets, guilt, resentment, and assigning blame. While you may not be missing a loved one, you may have lost many things like self-sufficiency, a life free of pain, economic security, a normal future, or hope of a long life. You no doubt have emotions to process and perhaps some unresolved relationships to deal with. Read Chapters 6–8 and complete the exercises for freedom and forgiveness as you apply those truths to your specific loss.

In Good Hands

The loss you are suffering has certainly affected your sense of security. The future may feel uncertain, and you may be struggling with emotional peace of mind. Read through Chapters 9–10, complete the Assignment "A Matter of Trust," and apply those truths to your life.

For What Purpose?

There may not be an apparent purpose for the pain you are going through right now, but there is a renewed purpose for you. Read Chapters 11–12, complete the Assignment "Sharing My Progress," and then apply it to your situation.

Helpful Resources

Letting go of all you have lost and moving forward to a new normal is challenging. Following are a few suggested resources designed to help you move forward.

Kate Jackson, "Grieving Chronic Illness and Injury—Infinite Losses," Social Work Today, July/August 2014, https://www. socialworktoday.com/archive/070714p18.shtml.

Angie Ebba, "Grieving for My Old Life after a Chronic Illness Diagnosis," Healthline, April 18,2019, https://www.healthline.com/health/grief-cycle-chronic-illness#1.

Barbara Okun and Joseph Nowinski, *Saying Goodbye: A Guide to Coping with a Loved One's Terminal Illness* (New York: Berkley Books, 2012).

* * * * *

Loss Due to Sexual Abuse

Sexual abuse can be one of the most devastating losses and emotionally damaging experiences a person can endure. It is a complete violation of one's personhood. It can result in feeling the loss of innocence, the loss of wholeness, the loss of trust, the loss of safety, protection, and security, the loss of personal value and self-worth, even the loss of control of your own body.

Sexual abuse wounds the whole person—body, soul, and spirit—at a deep level. While the grief recovery process offered in this book is applicable to sexual abuse victims, we urge you to seek personal counseling from someone experienced in helping those who have survived sexual abuse. If you elect to use this book to help you with your recovery process, please consider it to be a mere steppingstone toward getting professional help. Even the suggested resources at the end of this section are meant as a supplement to spending personal time with someone who can guide you through the difficult healing process.

You have experienced deep emotional wounds and need healing for a broken heart, renewed spiritual strength, a renewed sense of wholeness, emotional peace of mind, and a renewed sense of purpose. That is what the grieving and recovery process described in this book is designed to help you accomplish. Although in this book we have primarily applied the recovery process to the loss of a loved one, the truths that drive that process are equally applicable to many other emotional losses, including sexual abuse. But again, we suggest that you consider this process a supplement to seeking professional help.

We suggest you read through this book with a friend who will act as your journey partner. Together you will complete the Experiential exercises and apply them to your specific loss.

Your Need for Comfort

You have suffered loss on many levels. Your body has been violated. You have suffered emotional damage, and your spirit has been wounded. And that is where the healing ministry of comfort comes in.

Finish your reading of Chapter 2, and then go on to read Chapter 3, along with the accompanying Experiential exercises. As you read, apply the truths to your specific situation and receive needed comfort from God.

A Backlog of Hurts

After reading Chapter 4, complete the Assignment "A Chart of Past Hurts." Be sure to include any past hurts related to abusive relationships as a young person, violation of trust you may have experienced, and any other major losses. Mourn those losses—as well as your current loss—with your journey partner and openly receive comfort from him or her.

God Cares

God cares about what is happening in your life right now. You may have questions as to why you have to be suffering through your painful circumstances, yet God cares and hurts with you. Read Chapter 5, complete the Assignment "Can You Hear Me Now?," and apply it all to your situation.

Freedom and Forgiveness

You probably are struggling with regrets, false guilt, resentment, anger, and assigning blame. While you may not have lost a loved one, you have lost so many things, including the loss of emotional wholeness. Your sense of safety and security has been shaken. You have emotions to process involving unresolved relationship issues on a number of levels. Included within this mix are your feelings toward the person who violated you. You may even feel guilt, though you are not to blame.

Read Chapters 6–8 and complete the exercises for freedom and forgiveness as you apply those truths to your specific loss.

In Good Hands

The loss you have suffered has certainly affected your sense of security. The future may feel uncertain, and you are probably struggling to find emotional peace of mind. Read through Chapters 9–10, complete the Assignment "A Matter of Trust," and apply those truths to your life.

For What Purpose?

There may not be an apparent purpose for the pain you are going through right now, but there is a renewed purpose for you. Read Chapters 11–12, complete the Assignment "Sharing My Progress," and apply it to your situation.

Helpful Resources

Moving forward after sexual abuse is definitely a challenge. Following are a few suggested resources designed to help you move forward to a new normal. Your church may have recovery groups and counseling you will want to take advantage of. You need someone with experience in this area to guide you through the recovery process.

Louise Madill, "Sexual Abuse: The Healing Journey," Focus on the Family (Canada), 2010, https://www.focusonthefamily.ca/content/sexual-abuse-the-healing-journey.

Vanessa Marin, "How to Support a Friend or Loved One Who Has Been Sexually Abused," *The New York Times*, February 27, 2019, https://www.nytimes.com/2019/02/27/smarter-living/sexual-abuse-assault-support-mental-health.html.

Dan B. Allender, *Healing the Wounded Heart: The Heartache of Sexual Abuse and the Hope of Transformation* (Grand Rapids, MI: Baker Books, 1989).

Pain 2 Purpose Group Leaders Guide

The Purpose of the Book

The intention of *From Pain 2 Purpose* is to help a person who is suffering a major loss to begin a journey of grieving in a productive way so as to move forward in life and find a new normal. The problem is that most of us have not been taught how to grieve in a productive way. Consequently, we allow certain obstacles to mix in with our grief that hinder us from moving forward emotionally. This book is designed to help a person let go of those unproductive things to avoid becoming stuck in a continual cycle of unresolved grief.

This book is about embracing a series of repeated, relational choices on a journey that consists of letting go and continuing to let go of unproductive roadblocks to healing, such as regrets, guilt, anger, and fear. The journey also involves a corresponding series of repeated, relational choices that require the grieving person to hold on and keep holding on to productive assets, such as healing comfort, forgiveness, trust, and assurance that God truly cares and is with us.

Your task as a group leader is to be a gentle and caring guide to help initiate the letting go and holding on journey for those who have suffered a major loss. In doing this, you are initiating a ministry of hope and comfort to help bring healing to broken hearts, renewed spiritual strength, a renewed sense of wholeness, emotional peace of mind, and eventually a renewed sense of purpose.

How to Use This Material

This book is designed to be used by grieving people and their partners who have been chosen to journey with them. Each participant is to read through chapters of the book and then complete written and verbal exercises called "Assignments" and "Experientials" that occur in each section. The person suffering a loss responds in writing to the questions, which are designed to enable an assessment of where the person is in the journey toward healing and renewed hope. Then the grieving person and the partner are to meet and share openly what they have written and how they are processing their grief.

The group meetings you will conduct are vital to this process. You will be providing a place of hope and an atmosphere of emotional care and safety. Each partnering team of two will openly share what they are discovering together, which will result in all the participants mutually supporting the others in the group. This will create a sense that these grieving people are not alone in their difficult journey toward recovery.

As a group leader, you, too, may be suffering a major loss. If so, you will want to engage with a partner and complete each exercise prior to your group meeting. This will give you an opportunity to take the initiative and be the first to share openly what you personally are discovering.

The meetings you will conduct are based largely on the Assignments and Experientials (Encounter Jesus, Experience Scripture, and Engage in Fellowship exercises) within the book. There are three sections, titled as follows: "There Is Comfort for You to Receive," "There Are Promises for You to Claim," and "There Is a Purpose God Wants to Reveal." The Assignments and Experientials within these sections are designed to lead a person to experience the truth of Scripture and encounter the person of Jesus so he or she can find comfort and healing for a broken heart.

Each person will need to have a copy of *From Pain 2 Purpose*. So prior to the introductory meeting, be sure to order sufficient copies of the book. Go to: themullettfamily.com or greatcommandment.net/resources to place your order.

Conducting the Introductory Meeting

In this meeting, your group agrees to be part of the Pain 2 Purpose class based on this book. At this meeting, you will set a place and time for the six meetings.

Share the purpose for this course by explaining the purpose of this book, which is covered under the subheading appropriately named "The Purpose of the Book" on page 179. Explain that there are journaling exercises within the book called "Assignments" and "Experientials" that are Encounter Jesus, Experience Scripture, and Engage in Fellowship. The participants and their partners are to complete these exercises by engaging in times of prayer, devotion, and self-reflection, and record their feelings on pages provided in the book as they progress through the healing journey. These completed exercises will be discussed in each subsequent group meeting. Each meeting should last approximately one hour, not counting fellowship time prior to or after the meeting.

If any participants grieving a loss do not bring a partner to the meeting, discuss the need for them to seek someone out who will take the journey with them.

Pass out the books and explain that they are to read Chapters 1–3 and complete the first Section, "There Is Comfort for You to Receive." Close in prayer.

The First Pain 2 Purpose Meeting

Gently probe to determine how many partnering teams actually read Chapters 1–3 and completed the Assignments and Experientials. It is likely that some partnering teams will not have completed their reading and Experientials. During your session, you can allow them to withdraw to a more private space where they can work through the material together. Once they complete all or a portion of the Assignments and Experientials, ask them to share with the group as much information as they feel comfortable sharing. Follow this same procedure at each subsequent meeting.

Consider asking the group these questions:

1. What was your response to the idea of "letting go and holding on"? Do you sense that you have some things you need to let go of and hold on to? (Allow time for every partnering team to respond. Emphasize that grief recovery is not

a destination but rather a series of repeated, relational choices of letting go and holding on.)

2. Was there anything else in Chapter 1 that stood out to you?

3. Chapter 2 encouraged us to accept the reality that we are heartbroken and that we must choose to patiently endure the healing process. How has that been a challenge for you to accept?

4. Scripture says that "we belong to each other, and each needs all the others" (Romans 12:5 TLB). How difficult is it for you to accept emotional care from another person? (Discuss the truth that we know we need God, but we don't always realize that we also need one another to give us comfort for a broken heart.)

5. For you who are journey partners, did you get any fresh insight into what comfort is and isn't? (Discuss.)

6. Did anyone need to let go of a sense of unworthiness or self-reliance in order to receive comfort? (Discuss and point out that we need to let go of any sense of unworthiness and self-reliance we might have and hold on with gratefulness and humility to comfort that is being offered.)

7. Share your own experience of completing the Assignment and Experiential portions of the material. Then ask other partnering teams to share how working on the exercises went for them. (Specifically, ask for their response to how it makes them feel to know there is a comforting Jesus who weeps for them.)

As you close the meeting, mention the importance of reading Chapter 4 and completing the exercises prior to the next group meeting. Close in prayer.

The Second Pain 2 Purpose Meeting

Gently probe to determine how many partnering teams completed Chapter 4 and the exercises. This may be a difficult assignment for some to complete. But if at least one team completed the chapter, consider asking the following questions:

1. Share with us, to the extent you feel comfortable, how it went for you when you created your chart listing past hurts and the comfort you received. (Rejoice with those who report receiving comfort.)

2. Discuss the possible struggle you experienced in finding comfort for past losses. Also discuss your feelings about the importance of receiving that comfort. (Explain that if we haven't addressed our past hurts, those unresolved hurts build up a backlog of suffering in our lives. While those unresolved painful experiences remain in our past, we carry them into our present, and they negatively affect us. In fact, some of those major unhealed experiences can radiate into our present grief and hinder us from moving forward emotionally.)

3. Share your own experience of completing the Experiential exercises in the chapter. Then ask other partnering teams to share how completing the exercises went for them.

As you close the meeting, remind the group that in the next session they are to have read Chapter 5 and completed its Assignments and Experientials. Close in prayer.

The Third Pain 2 Purpose Meeting

Gently probe to determine how many partnering teams read the assignment and completed the exercises. Consider asking the group:

1. Have you struggled at all with the question of why you experienced this loss? Have you questioned why pain and suffering and death exist in this world? Have you

been angry that they do? (Assure the group that it's okay to struggle. Reference to section "Blinded to His Goodness" in Chapter 5 as needed.)

2. How does God feel about your loss? Do you think Jesus truly relates to what you are going through? How might this reality of a contemporary Jesus (who hurts for you) bring you hope? (Reference to section "He Truly Hurts When We Hurt" in Chapter 5 as needed.)

3. Discuss the need to let go of any anger and questioning of why God has allowed our suffering. Emphasize the need to hold on to the belief that God is truly good and that we can claim his promises as our own. What are some promises that you are currently holding on to? (Note the various scriptural promises identified in Chapter 5.)

4. Share your own experience of completing the Experiential exercises. Then ask if one or two partnering teams would share how it went as they completed the exercises.

As you close the meeting, remind the group that before the next session they are to read Chapters 6, 7, and 8 and complete the Assignment and Experientials. Close in prayer.

The Fourth Pain 2 Purpose Meeting

Gently probe to determine how many partnering teams have read Chapters 6–8 and completed the exercises. Consider asking the group:

1. No relationship is perfect or ever fully completed. So it was with the loved one you lost or other losses you have experienced. After having a relationship cut off while imperfect and incomplete, it's natural to feel a measure of guilt for what you perceive as your responsibility for the imperfection and incompleteness. Those if-onlys and not-enoughs plague you with regrets. We were asked to list some of our if-onlys and not-enoughs in the chapter. Who would be willing to share some of yours? (Share from your own experience first.)

2. The good news is that there is something that can free us from our guilt and regrets. What is it? (Reinforce that we can let go of our guilt and regrets and take hold of God's forgiveness. This allows his grace and mercy to flood our soul, even to the extent of enabling us to forgive ourselves.)

3. Make the point that we don't actually need people to respond to our seeking their forgiveness to be forgiven by God. Ask the group: Was that a refreshing truth to you? (See Chapter 7, section titled "The Power of Forgiveness.")

4. Did you find any freedom of forgiveness related to any guilt or regrets lingering from your imperfect relationship with your lost loved one or with others? Please share what you're comfortable sharing.

5. We may even need to forgive our loved one, spouse, or other significant person from some past hurt. Did anyone have some forgiving to do? (Reinforce that we can let go of any resentment, irritation, displeasure, dissatisfaction, or ill feelings we may have toward others. We can take hold of a forgiving spirit and forgive as we have been forgiven.)

6. The Experiential exercises in Chapter 8 are designed to facilitate more freedom and your choice of forgiveness. Share your own experience of completing these exercises. Then ask if one or two partnering teams would share how the "Engage in Fellowship" process worked for them.

As you close the meeting, remind the group that before the next session they are to have completed Chapters 9–10 and the Assignment and Experientials. Close in prayer.

The Fifth Pain 2 Purpose Meeting

Gently probe to determine how many partnering teams read Chapters 9–10 and completed the exercises. Consider asking the group:

1. After a major loss, it's natural to feel some anxiety and to fear what's going to happen next. Have you experienced any of that? Please share.

2. How do we find emotional peace of mind? (Ask someone in the group to read the first five Scripture passages found in the section titled "Security and Peace of Mind" from Chapter 9. They are John 14:27; John 16:32–33; Jeremiah 29:11–14; Psalm 94:19; and Psalm 34:6.) These passages assure us that God loves us and is really with us. When we truly believe this, we can begin to let go of anxieties and fear of the future and hold on to the assurance that God is with us no matter what.

3. It's not easy to keep trusting your future to God's hands when life feels unfair and out of control. Has life tended to feel unfair and out of control following the losses you have experienced? If so, what have you tended to do to counter that?

4. Ask someone to read 1 Peter 2:19–23. Then ask: How could Jesus entrust himself (leave his well-being) in God's hands when he was so mistreated and suffered unjustly on the cross? (Answer: Because Jesus believed his Father judged justly and ultimately had everything under control.) We must let go of the unproductive perspective that we control our own destiny and hold on to our trust that God has our present and eternal future in his hands.

5. Share your own experience of completing the Experiential exercises. Then ask if one or two partnering teams would share as they completed their Engage in Fellowship experiences.

As you close the meeting, remind the group to read Chapters 11–12 and complete the Assignment and Experientials by the next meeting. Close in prayer.

The Sixth Pain 2 Purpose Meeting

Gently probe to determine how many have read Chapters 11–12 and completed the exercises. Consider asking the group:

1. Ask someone to read Romans 8:28. What "good" is God working together in this passage? (We may see nothing good about death or other losses, but God is working circumstances together that produce good for us. Look at the section titled "Not Just Going through It, But Also Growing through It." Consider reading aloud the information beginning with the fourth paragraph and continuing through the rest of that section.)

2. This last "let go and hold on" may be the most difficult: We are called to let go of our past normal, offer God our present broken and shattered lives, and hold on to a new normal and renewed purpose that God will reveal. Ask: It may be too early to ask, but does anyone sense a renewed purpose that will serve others and give God honor and glory out of your broken and shattered life?

3. Grief recovery is an ongoing process. We don't let go of the cherished love and memories of our loved ones and losses. We must let go of our past normal and accept a new normal. Do you realize this is not a one-time letting go? We must repeatedly let go of those unproductive obstacles such as regrets, guilt, fear, and anger in order to keep moving forward. Are you at the point where you can realize that? (Discuss.)

4. To see where we are on our journey, let's go to Chapter 12 and read the section titled "Assessing Your Progress." There are seven areas to assess. We'll begin with the first one, which is "Receiving Comfort." Will someone read the two paragraphs under "Receiving Comfort"? Then let's each answer those questions as a way of assessing our progress thus far. (You take the lead and vulnerably answer the first set of questions. Once you complete the "Receiving Comfort" assessment with the

group, go on to "Backlog of Hurts" and continue through all seven sections. This will allow all participants to share where they are on their journey. Emphasize that we must avoid putting pressure on ourselves if we're not as far along as we hoped. We also need to resist feeling pressure from others.)

5. Remind those in your group that this is only the beginning. The journey of grief recovery is a series of repeated, relational choices that involve continually letting go and holding on. Some of those choices will be repeated, relational for a lifetime. (Discuss ways to stay connected and maintain a caring relationship with each other.)

6. Close in prayer.

Appendix 1

About the Great Commandment Network

The Great Commandment Network is a collaborative network of kingdom leaders who empower people to experience and reproduce great relationships through loving God and others (Matthew 22:37–40; 28:19–20).

The Great Commandment Network includes several strategic partners and initiatives:

- **Relationship Press:** This strategic team collaborates, supports, and joins together with churches, denominational partners, and professional associates to develop and produce resources that facilitate ongoing Great Commandment ministry.

- **Care4Pastors:** This initiative seeks to equip pastors who flourish, so they lead churches that thrive and then transform communities together.

- **The Galatians 6:6 Retreat Ministry:** This ministry offers a unique two-day retreat for ministers and their spouse. This gifted retreat is designed for personal renewal and reaffirming ministry and family priorities.

- **The Intimacy Therapy Network:** This group of professional therapists and relational coaches is committed to providing quality care for individuals, couples, and families from an Intimacy Therapy perspective.

- **Spirit-Empowered Faith:** This initiative reveals how it is only a deep, relational connection with our Savior that gives the experience and power to love God and love others well. The Spirit-empowered faith series of resources highlights forty specific outcomes that help measure and encourage spiritual growth.

- **Called2Love:** This initiative takes a relational message of how we are Called 2 Love God and people and pairs it with the practical methods and strategies to benefit couples, families, churches, and communities.

Appendix 2

A Spirit-Empowered Faith

Expresses Itself in Great Commission Living Empowered by Great Commandment Love

begins with the end in mind: The Great Commission calls us to make disciples.

"Go therefore and make disciples of all the nations, baptizing them in the name of the Father and the Son and the Holy Spirit teaching them to observe all that I have commanded you; and lo, I am with you always, even to the end of the age" (Matthew 28:19–20 NASB).

The ultimate goal of our faith journey is to relate to the person of Jesus because it is our relational connection to Jesus that will produce Christlikeness and spiritual growth. This relational perspective of discipleship is required if we hope to have a faith that is marked by the Spirit's power.

Models of discipleship that are based solely upon what we know and what we do are incomplete, lacking the empowerment of a life of loving and living intimately with Jesus. A Spirit-empowered faith is relational and impossible to realize apart from a special work of the Spirit. For example, the Spirit-empowered outcome of "listening to and hearing God" implies relationship—it is both relational in focus and requires the Holy Spirit's power to live.

begins at the right place: The Great Commandment calls us to start with loving God and loving others.

"'You shall love the Lord your God with all your heart, with all your soul, and with all your mind.' This is the first and foremost commandment. The second is like it: 'You shall love your neighbor as yourself.' On these two commandments depend the whole Law and the Prophets" (Matthew 22:37–40 NASB).

Relevant discipleship does not begin with doctrines or teaching, parables or stewardship—but with loving the Lord with all your heart, mind, soul, and strength and then loving the people closest to you. Since Matthew 22:37–40 gives us the first and greatest commandment, a Spirit-empowered faith starts where the Great Commandment tells us to start: A disciple must first learn to deeply love the Lord and to express his love to the "nearest ones"—his or her family, church, and community (and in that order).

embraces a relational process of Christlikeness.

"Walk while you have the light, lest darkness overtake you" (John 12:35 *ESV*).

Scripture reminds us that there are three sources of light for our journey: Jesus, his Word, and his people. The process of discipleship (or becoming more like Jesus) occurs as we relate intimately with each source of light.

Spirit-empowered discipleship will require a lifestyle of:

- Fresh encounters with Jesus (John 8:12)
- Frequent experiences of Scripture (Psalm 119:105)
- Faithful engagement with God's people (Matthew 5:14)

can be defined with observable outcomes using a biblical framework.

"And He Himself gave some to be apostles, some prophets, some evangelists, and some pastors and teachers, for the equipping of the saints for the work of ministry, for the edifying of the body of Christ" (Ephesians 4:11–12 NKJV).

The metrics for measuring Spirit-empowered faith or the growth of a disciple come from Scripture and are organized/framed around four distinct dimensions of a disciple who serves.

A relational framework for organizing Spirit-Empowered Discipleship outcomes draws from a cluster analysis of several Greek (diakoneo, leitourgeo, dou- leuo) and Hebrew words ('abad, Sharat), which elaborate on the Ephesians 4:12 declaration that Christ's followers are to be equipped for works of ministry or service. Therefore, the 40 Spirit Empowered Faith Outcomes have been identified and organized around:

- Serving/loving the Lord – While they were ministering to the Lord and fasting (Acts 13:2 NASB).[1]

- Serving/loving the Word – But we will devote ourselves to prayer and to the ministry of the Word (Acts 6:4 NASB).[2]

- Serving/loving people – Through love serve one another (Galatians 5:13 NASB).[3]

- Serving/loving his mission – Now all these things are from God, who reconciled us to himself through Christ and gave us the ministry of reconciliation (2 Corinthians 5:18 NASB).[4]

---

1   Ferguson, David L. Great Commandment Principle. Cedar Park, Texas: Relationship Press, 2013.
2   Ferguson, David L. Relational Foundations. Cedar Park, Texas: Relationship Press, 2004.
3   Ferguson, David L. Relational Discipleship. Cedar Park, Texas: Relationship Press, 2005.
4   "Spirit Empowered Outcomes," www.empowered21.com, Empowered 21 Global Council, http://empowered21.com/discipleship-materials/.

Appendix 3

A Spirit-Empowered Disciple

 A SPIRIT-EMPOWERED DISCIPLE LOVES THE LORD THROUGH

L1. Practicing thanksgiving in all things
"Enter the gates with thanksgiving" (Ps. 100:4). "In everything give thanks" (I Th. 5:18). "As sorrowful, yet always rejoicing" (II Cor. 6:10).

L2. Listening to and hearing God for direction and discernment
"Speak Lord, Your servant is listening" (I Sam. 3:8–9). "Mary…listening to the Lord's word, seated at his feet" (Lk.10:38–42). "Shall I not share with Abraham what I am about to do?" (Gen. 18:17). "His anointing teaches you all things" (I Jn. 2:27).

L3. Experiencing God as he really is through deepened intimacy with him
"Hear, O Israel: The Lord our God, the Lord is one. Love the Lord your God with all your heart and with all your soul and with all your strength" (Deut. 6:4,5). "Yet the Lord longs to be gracious to you; therefore he will rise up to show you compassion. For the Lord is a God of justice" (Is. 30:18). See also John 14:9.

L4. Rejoicing regularly in my identity as "His Beloved"
"And His banner over me is love" (Song of Sol. 2:4). "To the praise of the glory of His grace, which He freely bestowed on us in the beloved" (Eph. 1:6). "For the Lord gives to His beloved even in their sleep" (Ps. 127:2).

L5. Living with a passionate longing for purity and to please him in all things
"Who may ascend the hill of the Lord—he who has clean hands and a pure heart" (Ps. 24:3). "Beloved, let us cleanse ourselves from all of flesh and spirit, perfecting holiness in the fear of God" (II Cor. 7:1). "I always do the things that are pleasing to Him" (Jn. 8:29). "Though He slay me, yet will I hope in Him" (Job 13:15).

L6.   **Consistent practice of self-denial, fasting, and solitude rest**
"He turned and said to Peter, '"Get behind me, Satan! You are an obstacle to me. You are thinking not as God does, but as human beings do"' (Matt. 16:23). "But you when you fast…" (Mt. 6:17). "Be still and know that I am God" (Ps. 46:10).

L7.   **Entering often into Spirit-led praise and worship**
"Bless the Lord O my soul and all that is within me…" (Ps. 103:1). "Worship the Lord with reverence" (Ps. 2:11). "I praise Thee O Father, Lord of heaven and earth…" (Mt. 11:25).

L8.   **Disciplined, bold and believing prayer**
"Pray at all times in the Spirit" (Eph. 6:18). "Call unto me and I will answer…" (Jer. 33:3)). "If you ask according to His will—He hears—and you will have…" (I Jn. 5: 14–15).

L9.   **Yielding to the Spirit's fullness as life in the Spirit brings supernatural intimacy with the Lord, manifestation of divine gifts, and witness of the fruit of the Spirit**
"For by one Spirit we were all baptized into one body, whether Jews or Greeks, whether slaves or free, and we were all made to drink of one Spirit" (I Cor. 12:13). "You shall receive power when the Holy Spirit comes upon you" (Acts 1:8). "But to each one is given the manifestation of the Spirit for the common good" (I Cor. 12:7). See also, I Pet. 4:10, and Rom. 12:6.

L10.   **Practicing the presence of the Lord, yielding to the Spirit's work of Christlikeness**
"And we who with unveiled faces all reflect the Lord's glory, are being transformed into His likeness from glory to glory which comes from the Lord, who is the Spirit" (II Cor. 3:18). "As the deer pants after the water brooks, so my soul pants after You, O God" (Ps. 42:1).

A SPIRIT-EMPOWERED DISCIPLE LIVES THE WORD THROUGH

W1.   **Frequently being led by the Spirit into deeper love for the One who wrote the Word**
"Love the Lord thy God—love thy neighbor; upon these two commandments deepens all the law and prophets" (Mt. 22:37-40). "I delight in Your commands because I love them." (Ps. 119:47). "The ordinances of the Lord are pure—they are more precious than gold— sweeter than honey" (Ps. 19:9-10).

W2.   **Being a "living epistle" in reverence and awe as his Word becomes real in my life, vocation, and calling**
"You yourselves are our letter—known and read by all men" (II Cor. 3:2). "And the Word became flesh and dwelt among us" (Jn. 1:14). "Husbands love your wives—cleansing her by the washing with water through the Word" (Eph. 5:26). See also Tit. 2:5. "Whatever you do, do your work heartily, as for the Lord…" (Col. 3:23).

W3. Yielding to the Scripture's protective cautions and transforming power to bring life change in me
"I gain understanding from Your precepts; therefore I hate every wrong path" (Ps. 119:104). "Be it done unto me according to Your word" (Lk. 1:38). "How can a young man keep his way pure? By living according to Your word" (Ps. 119:9). See also Col. 3:16–17.

W4. Humbly and vulnerably sharing of the Spirit's transforming work through the Word
"I will speak of your statutes before kings and will not be put to shame" (Ps. 119:46). "Preach the word; be ready in season and out to shame" (II Tim. 4:2).

W5. Meditating consistently on more and more of the Word hidden in the heart
"I have hidden Your Word in my heart that I might not sin against You" (Ps. 119:12). "May the words of my mouth and the meditation of my heart be pleasing in Your sight, O Lord, my rock and my redeemer" (Ps. 19:14).

W6. Encountering Jesus in the Word for deepened transformation in Christlikeness
"All of us, gazing with unveiled face on the glory of the Lord, are being transformed into the same image from glory to glory, as from the Lord who is the Spirit" (II Cor. 3:18). "If you abide in Me and My words abide in you, ask whatever you wish, and it will be done for you" (Jn. 15:7). See also Lk. 24:32, Ps. 119:136, and II Cor. 1:20.

W7. A life-explained as one of "experiencing Scripture"
"This is that spoken of by the prophets" (Acts 2:16). "My comfort in my suffering is this: Your promise preserves my life" (Ps. 119:50). "My soul is consumed with longing for Your laws at all times" (Ps. 119:20).

W8. Living "naturally supernatural", in all of life, as his Spirit makes the written Word (*logos*) the living Word (*Rhema*)
"Faith comes by hearing and hearing by the Word (Rhema) of Christ" (Rom. 10:17). "Your Word is a lamp to my feet and a light for my path" (Ps. 119:105).

W9. Living abundantly "in the present" as his Word brings healing to hurt and anger, guilt, fear and condemnation—which are *heart hindrances* to life abundant
"The thief comes to steal, kill and destroy…" (John 10:10). "I run in the path of Your commands for You have set my heart free" (Ps. 119:32). "…and you shall know the truth and the truth shall set you free" (Jn. 8:32). "For freedom Christ set us free; so stand firm and do not submit again to the yoke of slavery" (Gal. 5:1).

W10. Implicit, unwavering trust that his Word will never fail
"The grass withers and the flower fades but the Word of God abides forever" (Is. 40:8). "So will My word be which goes forth from My mouth, it will not return to me empty" (Is. 55:11).

A SPIRIT-EMPOWERED DISCIPLE LOVES PEOPLE THROUGH

P1. **Living a Spirit-led life of doing good in all of life: relationships and vocation, community and calling**
"…He went about doing good…" (Acts 10:38). "Let your light shine before men in such a way that they may see your good works, and glorify your Father who is in heaven" (Mt. 5:16). "But love your enemies, and do good, and lend, expecting nothing in return, and your reward will be great, and you will be sons of the Most High; for He Himself is kind to ungrateful and evil men" (Lk. 6:35). See also Rom. 15:2.

P2. **Startling people with loving initiatives to give *first***
"Give, and it will be given to you. They will pour into your lap a good measure—pressed down, shaken together, and running over. For by your standard of measure it will be measured to you in return" (Lk. 6:38). "But Jesus was saying, 'Father, forgive them; for they do not know what they are doing.' (Lk. 23:34). See also Lk. 23:43 and Jn. 19:27.

P3. **Discerning the relational needs of others with a heart to give of his love**
"Let no unwholesome word proceed from your mouth, but only such a word as is good for edification according to the need of the moment, so that it will give grace to those who hear" (Eph. 4:29). "And my God will supply all your needs according to His riches in glory in Christ Jesus" (Phil. 4:19). See also Lk. 6:30.

P4. **Seeing people as needing BOTH redemption from sin AND intimacy in relationships, addressing both human fallenness and aloneness**
"But God demonstrates His own love toward us, in that while we were yet sinners, Christ died for us" (Rom. 5:8). "When Jesus came to the place, He looked up and said to him, 'Zaccheus, hurry and come down, for today I must stay at your house'" (Lk. 19:5). See also Mk. 8:24 and Gen. 2:18.

P5. **Ministering his life and love to our *nearest ones* at home and with family as well as faithful engagement in his Body, the church**
"You husbands in the same way, live with your wives in an understanding way, as with someone weaker, since she is a woman; and show her honor as a fellow heir of the grace of life, so that your prayers will not be hindered" (I Pet. 3:7). See also I Pet. 3:1 and Ps. 127:3.

P6. **Expressing the fruit of the Spirit as a lifestyle and identity**
"But the fruit of the Spirit is love, joy, peace, patience, kindness, goodness, faithfulness, gentleness, self-control…" (Gal. 5:22-23). "With the fruit of a man's mouth his stomach will be satisfied; He will be satisfied with the product of his lips" (Prov. 18:20).

P7. **Expecting and demonstrating the supernatural as his spiritual gifts are made manifest and his grace is at work by his Spirit**
"In the power of signs and wonders, in the power of the Spirit; so that from Jerusalem and round about as far as Illyricum I have fully preached the gospel of Christ" (Rom. 15:19). "Truly, truly, I say to you, he who believes in Me, the works that I do, he will do also…" (Jn. 14:12). See also I Cor. 14:1.

P8. **Taking courageous initiative as a peacemaker, reconciling relationships along life's journey**

"…Live in peace with one another" (I Th. 5:13). "For He Himself is our peace, who made both groups into one and broke down the barrier of the dividing wall" (Eph. 2:14). "Therefore, confess your sins to one another, and pray for one another so that you may be healed. See also Jas. 5:16 and Eph. 4:31–32.

P9. **Demonstrating his love to an ever growing network of "others" as he continues to challenge us to love "beyond our comfort"**

"The one who says, 'I have come to know Him,' and does not keep His commandments, is a liar, and the truth is not in him" (I Jn. 2:4). "If someone says, 'I love God,' and hates his brother, he is a liar; for the one who does not love his brother whom he has seen, cannot love God whom he has not seen" (I Jn. 4:20).

P10. **Humbly acknowledging to the Lord, ourselves, and others that it is Jesus in and through us who is loving others at their point of need**

"Take My yoke upon you and learn from Me, for I am gentle and humble in heart, and you will find rest for your souls" (Mt. 11:29). "If I then, the Lord and the Teacher, washed your feet, you also ought to wash one another's feet" (Jn. 13:14).

A SPIRIT-EMPOWERED DISCIPLE LIVES HIS MISSION THROUGH

M1. **Imparting the gospel and one's very life in daily activities and relationships, vocation and community**

"Having so fond an affection for you, we were well-pleased to impart to you not only the gospel of God but also our own lives, because you had become very dear to us" (I Th. 2:8-9). See also Eph. 6:19.

M2. **Expressing and extending the Kingdom of God as compassion, justice, love, and forgiveness are shared**

"I must preach the kingdom of God to the other cities also, for I was sent for this purpose'" (Lk. 4:43). "As You sent Me into the world, I also have sent them into the world"(Jn. 17:18). "Restore to me the joy of Your salvation and sustain me with a willing spirit. Then I will teach transgressors Your ways, and sinners will be converted to you" (Ps. 51:12–13). See also Mic. 6:8.

M3. **Championing Jesus as the only hope of eternal life and abundant living**

"There is no salvation through anyone else, nor is there any other name under heaven given to the human race by which we are to be saved" (Acts 4:12). "A thief comes only to steal and slaughter and destroy; I came so that they might have life and have it more abundantly" (Jn. 10:10). See also Acts 4:12, Jn. 10:10, and Jn. 14:6.

M4. Yielding to the Spirit's role to convict others as he chooses, resisting expressions of condemnation
"And He, when He comes, will convict the world concerning sin and righteousness and judgment…" (Jn. 16:8). "Who is the one who condemns? Christ Jesus is He who died, yes, rather who was raised, who is at the right hand of God, who also intercedes for us" (Rom. 8:34). See also Rom. 8:1.

M5. Ministering his life and love to the "least of these"
"Then He will answer them, 'Truly I say to you, to the extent that you did not do it to one of the least of these, you did not do it to Me'" (Mt. 25:45). "Pure and undefiled religion in the sight of our God and Father is this: to visit orphans and widows in their distress, and to keep oneself unstained by the world" (Jas. 1:27).

M6. Bearing witness of a confident peace and expectant hope in God's Lordship in all things
"Now may the Lord of peace Himself continually grant you peace in every circumstance. The Lord be with you all!" (II Thess. 3:16). "Let the peace of Christ rule in your hearts, to which indeed you were called in one body; and be thankful" (Col. 3:15). See also Rom. 8:28 and Ps. 146:5.

M7. Faithfully sharing of time, talent, gifts, and resources in furthering his mission
"Of this church I was made a minister according to the stewardship from God bestowed on me for your benefit, so that I might fully carry out the preaching of the word of God" (Col. 1:25). "From everyone who has been given much, much will be required; and to whom they entrusted much, of him they will ask all the more" (Lk. 12:48). See also I Cor. 4:1–2.

M8. Attentive listening to others' *story*, vulnerably sharing of our story, and a sensitive witness of Jesus' story as life's ultimate hope; developing your story of prodigal, pre-occupied and pain-filled living; listening for other's story and sharing Jesus' story
"…but sanctify Christ as Lord in your hearts, always being ready to make a defense to everyone who asks you to give an account for the hope that is in you, yet with gentleness and reverence" (I Pet. 3:15). "…because this son of mine was dead, and has come to life again" (Luke 11:24). (Mark 5:21–42). (Jn. 9:1–35).

M9. Pouring our life into others, making disciples who in turn make disciples of others
"Go therefore and make disciples of all nations, baptizing them in the name of the Father and the Son and the Holy Spirit, teaching them to observe all that I commanded you; and lo, I am with you always, even to the end of the age" (Mt. 28:19–20). See also II Tim. 2:2.

M10. Living submissively within his Body, the Church, as instruction and encouragement, reproof and correction are graciously received by faithful disciples
"…and be subject to one another in the fear of Christ" (Eph. 5:21). "Brethren, even if anyone is caught in any trespass, you who are spiritual, restore such a one in a spirit of gentleness; each one looking to yourself, so that you too will not be tempted" (Gal. 6:1). See also Gal. 6:2.

Endnotes

1   Douglas Brinkley, as quoted by Marco della Cava, "America Has Suffered Great Loss Before. Here's How We May Learn to Cope with Coronavirus Death Toll," *USA Today*, April 17, 2020, https://www.usatoday.com/story/news/nation/2020/04/17/coronavirus-death-toll-vietnam-spanish-flu-loss/2985542001/.

2   Gary Roe, *Please Be Patient, I'm Grieving: How to Care for and Support the Grieving Heart* (Wellborn, TX: Healing Resources Publishing, 2016), 44.

3   H. Norman Wright, *Experiencing Grief* (Nashville, TN: B&H Publishing Group, 2004), 79.

4   "Post-Traumatic Stress Disorder," *National Institute of Mental Health*, May 2019, https://www.nimh.nih.gov/health/topics/post-traumatic-stress-disorder-ptsd/index.shtml.

5   "The Connection between Physical & Emotional Pain," Southside Pain Specialists, February 7, 2019, https://www.southsidepainspecialists.com/the-connection-between-physical-and-emotional-pain/.

6   David Augsburger, *Caring Enough to Forgive* (Ventura, CA: Regal Books, 1981), 48.

7   Marc Forster, dir., *Christopher Robin*, screenplay by Alex Ross Perry and Allison Schroeder, Walt Disney Pictures, 2018.

8   Nils Salzgeber, "29 Scientifically Proven Benefits of Gratitude You Don't Want to Miss," NJlifehacks, June 19, 2018, https://www.njlifehacks.com/gratitude-benefits.

Acknowledgments

Our first and foremost acknowledgement and heartfelt praise goes to our Storm-Chaser, Waymaker, Pain-Taker, Fire-Walker, and Eternal Reward. We are committed to you forever.

We are truly a reflection of those who've poured into our lives and ministered to us during our darkest nights.

Our parents planted the gift of faith into our hearts. We are forever grateful for the many sacrifices they, and each of our siblings, made for us during the countless hospital stays. We are blessed with the best families ever.

We would like to thank our precious children for being our heroes. You have chosen supernatural grace over and over again. We are stronger today and amazingly blessed because of the gift of each of you.

We have been humbled by the many pastors, individuals, and churches who have poured into our family's lives. There are too many to begin naming. Because of our prison ministry focus, our "family" has expanded to include many incarcerated brothers and sisters in Christ. Many of you have also become our heroes. It has been a great joy to share Jesus with you and to grow together. You continue to fill our hearts with more than we can give. Finding purpose in our pain has connected our hearts.

Someone once shared that our family had to become "one of the least of these" before we could effectively reach and minister to "the least of these." It has been a hard but breathtaking journey. One in which we continue to walk.

We are thankful for the guidance and vision Dave Bellis has provided us. He has poured his very heart into this project, and his many talents have truly been a gift from God. Dave and Becky have become dear friends of ours, and we know God allowed our paths to cross for a specific purpose. We will forever be grateful for this sweet couple.

It is a wonderful privilege to coauthor this project with Dr. David Ferguson and the Great Commandment Network and to be a small part of their incredible, life-changing ministry. David and Teresa Ferguson have impacted many lives across America and around the world. Dr. Ferguson is a spiritual giant that we so admire. He truly loves and exemplifies the Word of God. We are humbled to partner with Great Commandment Network in this way. The practical biblical truths and applications we have received from their ministry have forever changed our family.

We would also like to acknowledge and thank Terri Snead, Tom Williams, and Joan Williams for their valuable contributions and expertise in this book. We could not have done it without you.

BroadStreet Publishing deserves to be acknowledged for their excellent work in getting this message of hope into the lives of those who are hurting.

Our very breaths begin and end because of the Father and the Son. So should our praises. Thank you, Lord, for the beauty you create from our shattered dreams, broken hearts, and surrendered will. You are the sole reason we have found purpose in our pain. The blood oozing from your own pain spills deeply into our wounds yet offers new life and hope to each parched, broken soul.

Duane & Cindy Mullett

About the Authors

Duane and Cindy Mullett and their singing family have been involved in full time church and prison ministry, touring across the US and Canada for over thirty years. During these years of ministry, they have battled many life-threatening events with their children, including three heart transplants, two malignant cancers and other chronic conditions, as well as the eventual death of their oldest and only son, Austin.

As a touring, singing family, they not only have performed in concerts, they have conducted seminars on grief recovery. Out of their own grief recovery, the Mulletts have imparted a *From Pain 2 Purpose* life message to hundreds of churches and thousands of individuals, offering hope and healing to many.

Duane and Cindy have four children (all of whom sing on tour with the family). They reside in western North Carolina.

Dr. David Ferguson has helped to bring about emotional and spiritual health to believers for more than forty years.

As Executive Director of the Great Commandment Network, he serves over forty denominations and para-church ministries through pastoral care, training strategies, and resource development. In addition to authoring over thirty books, David has trained thousands of pastors and ministry couples in more than fifty countries of the world.

Together with his wife, Teresa, they have three children, seven special grandchildren, and three great-grandchildren. They reside in Austin, Texas.